WHITE SQUALL

THE LAST VOYAGE
OF
ALBATROSS

RICHARD E. LANGFORD

Editor: Jerry Renninger

Bristol Fashion Publications, Inc.
Harrisburg, Pennsylvania

White Squall -- *Richard Langford*

Published by Bristol Fashion Publications

ISBN: 1-892216-36-1
LCCN: 00-136119

Contribution acknowledgments

Inside Graphics: Richard Langford
Cover Design: John P. Kaufman
Cover Photo: Richard Langford

White Squall -- Richard Langford

White Squall -- *Richard Langford*

For Spook

"May the deep where he sleeps rock him gently, gently, until the end of time."

Joseph Conrad

Prologue

Back in 1960 I answered an ad in *Yachting* Magazine, placed by The Ocean Academy Ltd. owned and operated by Christopher B. Sheldon, Ph.D., and N. Alice Sheldon, MD. They wanted a teacher of English for a nine-month voyage on the school ship *Albatross*, a square-rigged brig to be crewed by teen-aged students.

The Sheldons expected to sail through the Caribbean, transit the Panama Canal, then spend a month or more in the Galapagos Islands before returning to their home port of Mystic, Conn. I was 35 years old, teaching English at Stetson University in DeLand, Fla., when I answered the ad. I was determined to sail on *Albatross*'s first schooling voyage even if obliged to resign from Stetson. Fortunately, an understanding dean and department head allowed me a leave of absence. As many readers no doubt know, the first schooling voyage of *Albatross* was also her last. This is the tale of that voyage.

I wrote most of it in the middle '60s, then put it aside for the interim. The film *White Squall* engendered fresh interest in the *Albatross* voyage, even though the film was more Hollywood parody than fact. Readers of this volume will acquire a more realistic understanding of the people and events involved.

I am indebted to travel writer Janet Groene for her interest in this book. She read it, liked it and recommended it to one of her publishers. Without her efforts on my behalf, the manuscript would remain in a box beneath my desk, where it had been for more than three decades.

Richard E. Langford

White Squall -- *Richard Langford*

chapter one
THE SHIP

I first saw *Albatross* in June 1960. She lay alongside a wharf at Mystic Seaport, Conn., her long bowsprit almost touching the stern of *Charles W. Morgan*, the old whaler now permanently moored there as an exhibit. *Albatross'* captain, Christopher Sheldon, had already hired me to serve as English Master for his ship's first schooling cruise, beginning the following fall, and I looked forward to seeing the vessel I would live aboard for nine months.

Albatross was 92 feet long, drew nine feet in the bow and 11 in the stern, and was rigged as a hermaphrodite brigantine: four squaresails on the foremast and a marconi main. She had teak decks, a 21-foot beam that gave ample deck space, a galley house on deck forward and a chart house aft. Painted white, trimmed in red and black with a beautiful mahogany stern rail that gleamed with varnish, she was the largest sailing ship I had seen up close. She had served as a North Sea pilot schooner following her commissioning in 1921 before conversion to a brigantine.

Chris and Alice Sheldon bought *Albatross* from novelist Ernest K. Gann, author of best sellers such as *The High and the Mighty, Soldier of Fortune* and *Twilight for the Gods.* Used by the Nazi Kriegsmarine during WW II, the ship was sold to a Dutch company in 1949, from which Gann bought her in 1954.

Gann had *Albatross* re-rigged as a brigantine, and though this probably affected her stability, he assured the Sheldons it did not. In any event, *Albatross* became a suitable romantic setting for the writer's adventure novels.

When the Sheldons bought *Albatross*, ship's cook George Ptacnik came with her. George was an intelligent, educated 30-year-old Mexican-American teacher of English who found *Albatross* far more appealing than the classroom. By the time I came aboard, George (who later became known as Spook) had already sailed with the Sheldons on an adventure cruise through the Mediterranean and around Africa.

Standing alongside, I craned back my head to see the tops of her masts. They looked like giant steel trees with white branches in the clouds, fitting perfectly with all the old sailing vessels surrounding her in Mystic Seaport harbor.

No one was on deck. I walked to the gangway and shouted, but there was no answer. Stepping aboard, I stuck my head through the aft companionway into the chart house and called out again. This time I got an answer, and Skipper Sheldon came on deck from the engine room where he had been working. He was a big man, about 6'2" and heavy through the midsection, with blond hair balding in front. His eyes were a startling blue.

I introduced myself and we sat on the aft-deck lockers. As we talked, I looked around at the bulwarks, the big wheel, the engine-room telegraph, the large compass and the wheelhouse. Albatross needed some red lead and paint, and what I could see of the mainsail did not encourage me regarding the ship's condition.

Sheldon read my expression. "We're taking her to Nova Scotia this summer for yard work." he said. "We just returned from Africa and a year at sea, and right now she's not up to par, but she will be by the time you see her this fall."

As I was to find out in a few months, even after the work in Nova Scotia *Albatross* required constant hard labor to keep her looking decent, more work than most of her young students had expected to perform.

Albatross took on supplies, tons of canned goods, crates of fresh vegetables, coils of new line stacked all around her well-worn decks. Skipper pointed to a high pile of canvas on top of the charthouse. "That's our new main. The old one is about gone, and I expect it will blow out almost anytime." Later that afternoon I helped feed the new main through the skylights down into the main cabin where we packed it away in one of the vacant bunks.

I explored the ship above and below. *Albatross* had a private stern cabin where Skipper and his wife lived, and it spanned the width of the ship. A narrow passageway led into the large main cabin where there were bunks for twelve. The dining table, in gimbals, was in the main cabin as well, while at the aft end was the ship's library (about 10 large shelves of books). Forward of the main cabin were 10 more bunks and several wash stands with two heads off the forepeak

As I climbed up the ladder out of the forepeak I heard a feminine voice say, "Hi. Welcome aboard." It was Alice Sheldon, the ship's surgeon, a handsome, heavyset woman of about 30 years. She smiled, and her short, brown hair blew about her face in the breeze. She spoke authoritatively and surely; I could tell that she was a very important part of the whole venture, and a few minutes of conversation with her told me that hers was the organizational mind that kept the Ocean Academy Ltd. moving smoothly.

John Perry (whose name soon became simply J.C.) had been hired a few days before as math teacher, and we worked together to stow our gear in our compartment. Alice had hung a heavy curtain between us and several of the boys so we had a semi-private area. We each had two bunks, one for sleeping and one for stowing books and other teaching materials.

Most of the students would come aboard in Bermuda, but Rick, Bill and Tim were already aboard, as well as several friends of the Sheldons who had sailed with them on Irving Johnson's *Yankee* a few years before. Our cook Spook was there, of course, and in just a few days, J.C., Spook and I had become good friends. At 35, I was the oldest person aboard Albatross; J.C. was 27, Spook was 30, and Skipper Sheldon was 34.

We rode out Hurricane Donna at Mystic Seaport. Though the Seaport wharves were under water and we had some wind and rain, there wasn't much damage. Skipper had us put out an extra anchor astern in the river and another on land.

Spook once described J.C. as "a loud, wild-eyed German storm trooper with an insane giggle," but it was said with a smile. Our math teacher was indeed loud-voiced, but he was also smart, confident, quick-witted and a skillful math teacher. He adapted quickly to the ship and became the mate of one of the three watches.

The final moments before we sailed from Mystic Seaport were hectic. The pilot and Skipper stood atop the charthouse as *Albatross* backed from her berth, swung, and headed down the Mystic River toward the town bridge. As we passed beneath it, Spook's laundry came bombing down on deck. (He had forgotten to pick it up, but a hasty phone call arranged for it to be delivered in this extraordinary fashion.)

We were under way.

chapter two
EN ROUTE

Sailing to Bermuda was exciting. Hurricane Donna had left the Atlantic with heavy swells and large following waves that kept *Albatross* on her scuppers most of the way. On the third day the mainsail blew out with a great, loud bang that awakened me about 2 a.m. There was much shouting and scrambling around on deck but Skipper did not sound All Hands, so I rolled over and went back to sleep. Next morning we bent on the new main; it was about all we could do to wrestle it topside, and the ship rolled like an old tug until we got it in place. Then she steadied back down on a port tack and plunged on at about eight knots toward Bermuda.

Spook performed pure magic in the galley through all the rough weather, serving up gourmet meals with fresh salads, casseroles, pancakes, pies, fresh doughnuts, cakes — even baked snapper and tuna. *Albatross'* old stove burned diesel fuel and was sometimes hard to get hot enough to work with, but Spook managed miracles.

Though it took a while, the ship and I finally came to terms. I agreed to stop banging it with my head if it would stop knocking me down and sliding me across the deck. J. C., a strong young man, had his troubles, too, rarely coming up without massaging his balding head where he had given it a good bump on the overhead. Both of us needed a few days to become accustomed to sleeping in the concrete mixer that was *Albatross'* forward section. It was bunkboards all the way, with braced knees and arms just to stay in bed as the ship pitched, rose, plowed and rolled. Alice consoled us by repeating that this was probably the worst weather we'd have on the trip.

After raising Bermuda following seven days at sea, it was still rainy and gusty when we dropped anchor about midnight in St. George Harbor. Next morning, Skipper sent me ashore in the dinghy so he'd have a man there to handle lines when he put the ship along the wharf. After I had rowed in, he decided it was too windy to risk *Albatross* in tight quarters.

The rain came down in sheets, and the wind was cold despite protection from my foul-weather gear. In a shed by the wharf I sheltered with three or four locals drinking rum and smoking. Invited to join them, I produced a dry cigar from an inside pocket, accepted a large paper cup of dark rum and sat down with them to wait out the rain. When the weather let up an hour later, I rowed back to *Albatross*. Skipper asked where I'd been for so long, and I told him I'd found some friends ashore with whom I had passed the time very pleasantly. When the skies cleared later, we put in at the St. George Dinghy Club, where the members made us welcome and let us use their bar and showers.

Within a few days the rest of the students came aboard,

a decidedly mixed lot from 15 to 18 and ranging from a couple of juvenile delinquents to several young pillars of the community. In intellect they ran the gamut from dullard to very bright.

J.C. and I soon discovered we had complicated jobs: we had to design courses in English, math, American history and German for students on the 10th, 11th, 12th grades and college-freshman levels. Some classes had seven or eight students, others only one or two. To make matters more difficult, the ship itself competed with us. Not only did the boys sail her but were expected to spend most of their spare time chipping rust, painting and otherwise maintaining *Albatross*. As a result, the crew was constantly tired because of physical labors or infrequent free afternoons of scuba diving, swimming, fishing, hiking, etc. Persuading them to study at night or pay attention in class wasn't easy.

Lessons were conducted mornings in the main cabin, in Skipper's cabin (he taught Spanish and celestial navigation), on deck (where Alice taught biology) and in the charthouse, where I taught history and English. In addition to my regular classes, Skipper asked me to teach both remedial and speed reading to all the students (Alice took the reading course, too), plus a Red Cross Senior Lifesaving course. I taught lifesaving in various ports and at beaches along the journey through the Caribbean, finally finishing the course with six lads on Bequia several months after it had begun on Tortola. It must have been the only certified Senior Lifesaving course ever conducted aboard a windjammer.

We all worked pretty hard on the ship in Bermuda, besides accomplishing a month of classes. Much sail mending had to be done, along with chipping rust, painting, sanding and varnishing. I put in many hours making canvas chafing gear for the main spreaders and re-canvassing several deck chairs. All in all it was pleasant enough; Bermuda was lovely, the weather warm and sunny, and each evening before supper there was the St. George Dinghy Club where adults could congregate, toss darts and enjoy a rum collins or two.

In time the boys began to learn the lines and the sail plan, and most had gone aloft often enough to set the squaresails and overcome any initial fear of heights. Accordingly, we mounted a few overnight cruises out of St. George in order to accustom them to handling *Albatross* at sea. Once we even took along Sir Julian Gascoigne, the governor of Bermuda. He had a fine time of it and handled the wheel like an experienced seaman.

With so many unique personalities aboard, each facing new tasks and fresh experiences daily, it was a complicated matter to administer discipline fairly. Rick, a good-natured, grinning 16-year-old from California, had a helpful and enthusiastic nature. He also had the foulest mouth I'd ever heard. He gloried in sailing and fishing, performing his galley work and ship's duties willingly, but his schoolwork was done only if nothing else were available. We always knew when Rick was near; obscenities flowed as if they were his first language and English his second. Sixteen-year-old Tod had little interest in anything other than chances to meet girls from port to port. He was a thin, dark-haired, sullen boy, crafty and sneaky, a born manipulator. He later fulfilled his destiny as an arrogant cheat by stealing an article of mine and publishing it as his own. Chuck could never seem to work or study enough to suit himself. An intense and serious redhead, Chuck became John Goodlett's best friend and they spent many hours together, on the ship and ashore. John, 18, worked hard, and his natural curiosity and physical ability soon earned him a mate's position. The 16-year-old first mate Bill was a dedicated soul who tried to learn everything to be known about a sailing vessel. He ran tight watches and work details, which did not make him popular with the lazier boys. He was an excellent first mate, however, and often gave up chances to go ashore to chip rust, turn-and-serve a new foot rope or study his school lessons.

And then there was Terry. J.C. and I felt sorry for his many inadequacies one day and could barely control our anger on the next as he performed one stupid trick after another. Just 16, he made no bones about the fact that he was aboard

Albatross in lieu of being in a California reform school. Terry was bright but had the attention span of a two-year-old. A creature of impulse, he was easily led by some of the older boys into scrapes aboard and ashore. Terry often played sycophant to 18-year-old Phil, an angry, defiant snob and not a good example for anyone to pattern himself after.

Tad was tough to get to know. His every act and gesture cried out for attention and approval, but his facade of couldn't-care-less about books, sailing and the world in general made it almost impossible to help him very much. He ended the trip more withdrawn than when he came aboard at Bermuda.

One of the most active and interested boys was Mike. At 16, big, enthusiastic and bright, he got along with everyone. Mike worked out part of his tuition as a "galley slave," and in the process of scrubbing Spook's dirty pots and pans, would shout, "My father sold me into slavery!" Mike's protestations always got a smile.

Tim was also a galley slave, a pleasant, smart kid who fit in well, and enjoyed the voyage. Bob was shy and introspective when he came aboard, but after a few months away from home, he opened up and became an outgoing young man who enjoyed himself. Just 15, he matured aboard ship and became a good sailor. Another 15-year-old was Dick, not one of the brighter boys on *Albatross,* Dick had to study hard to keep up, but he was generally a happy boy who participated eagerly in any new adventure. Robin was a fine, intelligent, serious boy who loved to talk and fish. He asked good questions and I could not always answer him. He enjoyed himself, and although he knew nothing about sailing when he boarded *Albatross,* he became a good sailor. Tom did not want to be on the ship at all in the beginning, and more than once he asked to be sent home. But he got over his homesickness eventually and took an interest in the ship. He became a fair carpenter and sailmaker before the voyage had ended. Chris from Canada was already a well-adjusted, fine young man when the trip began. He was intelligent, anticipated each day with pleasure, learned his shipboard duties very quickly, and was one of the two or three truly competent, confident boys I taught. Chris was 18 and had had sailing experience before he joined Albatross. His patience as a fisherman paid off in many excellent meals for all our crew.

For some, *Albatross* proved to be the right place in the long run. For most, it only pointed up and emphasized their inadequacies. Many needed some skill for which they could be recognized. They needed to become individuals, and if they could contend with the myriad pressures of life aboard a sailing vessel, it was good for them.

One of the rewarding features of being aboard *Albatross* was the chance for the boys to find out who they were, to become real people. Some shed their childish ways and turned into young men before the voyage ended. Others had to wait until *Albatross* slipped beneath the waves before they understood that no one lives forever, that every day and every experience is valuable, that selfishness and egoism are wasteful vanities that in the end come to nothing.

chapter three
THE WEST INDIES

Albatross left Bermuda in October and headed south to visit dozens of beautiful Dutch, English and French ports in the Leeward and Windward Islands. Our port of entry was Tortola, BWI, where we anchored in the harbor among other sailing craft, mostly native trading schooners.

Most of the crew came aboard with complete scuba equipment, and we had a gasoline-powered compressor on deck to recharge the air tanks. The compressor broke down regularly, though, and the boys spent more time repairing than using it. It finally quit completely, and everybody gave up on it except Terry, who spent hours tinkering with it week after week. Truth be told, most of the adults were glad to have it stop for good; the compressor made a horrible racket whenever someone infrequently coaxed it into operating, and some of us thought the use of gasoline on deck was dangerous. After one or two dives, most found they enjoyed using just their flippers and masks; they had all the freedom they needed without the cumbersome tanks and regulators. Only once did we have occasion to dive below 15 or 20 feet. In a tiny Caribbean cove, somebody accidentally dropped the Seagull outboard motor into 10 fathoms, and Skipper retrieved it with scuba equipment.

The adults called one evening at Fort Burt, Millie and Chris Hammersley's delightful hotel and bar that overlooked the bay. It was my introduction to society in the Caribbean and altogether an exciting evening. The bar looked like something out of a Somerset Maugham South Seas novel with straw matting on the walls and ceiling, wide rattan chairs and stools, an old-fashioned ceiling fan revolving slowly above us, and the clacking of palm fronds swaying in the sea breeze just outside the wide-open screenless windows. A big yellow moon hung high over the water and shed its tropical gold on the two or three people who sat on the verandah.

Millie Hammersley was in fine form, arguing with some Scotsman who was there to build a road. She preferred horses and resented the invasion of bulldozers and automobiles. Her husband Chris was a genial host, courteous and quiet, and made us all feel we were guests visiting a friendly private home. A very old lady glided into the room wearing a light blue gown that must have been in style in the Victorian era. She sat regally in one of the huge rattan peacock chairs; the flaring back framed her serious, disapproving expression in such a way that she resembled a cameo. She remained silent, and as far as I could tell, she said nothing during the two hours she was there. In the end she arose slowly and carefully, then glided out of the room.

J.C., Spook and I acquired our nicknames that night as

we were on our way back to *Albatross*. The three of us (I was leading the way) descended a winding path toward the harbor with Skipper and Alice following a little way behind. I paused to point my cane at our ship riding at anchor in the moonlit bay. She looked like an 18th-century pirate vessel home from battle.

John Perry laughed and shouted, "You look like Moses with that beard and cane, Langford! Lead on!"

"Lead on, Father," called Skipper from above.

"Yeah, Big Daddy, guide us home," offered Spook.

Then it fell into place for all of us. John, George and I had become something of a trio, and Skipper put it into words, calling, "Behold the Trinity! Big Daddy, J.C. and the Spook: the Father, the Son, and the Holy Ghost!" Our raucous laughter must have aroused half of Tortola, but the three names stuck for the rest of the voyage.

Before long, all the crew had nicknames except Alice and Skipper. Most of the boys were pleased with theirs and responded readily to them, almost as if each was willing to shed an old personality for a fresh one. In many ways the trip was a new life, a second chance for everybody. Some took advantage of it but many were not able to do so. Their personalities had been rigidly formed, and they often met new scenes and situations with old reactions that did not work.

Albatross cruised the Caribbean for more than five months until well after Christmas, stopping at remote, uninhabited islands, busy ports and large cities such as Fort de France in Martinique and Port of Spain in Trinidad. The boys learned the functions of approximately 100 lines aboard ship and became good sail handlers. Anytime we anchored or docked, we held classes in the mornings, while afternoons were given over to ship work or swimming, snorkeling, hiking, sailing the longboats and sightseeing.

After a few weeks everyone stopped wearing sneakers and went barefoot. The soles of our feet became like leather as a result of walking the wood decks and climbing the ratlines. Most eventually got to the point where they could sleep comfortably almost anywhere other than a bunk.

We spent a memorable day and night at Peter Island near Tortola, where we enjoyed our first powder-soft Caribbean beach, gin-clear water, light-yellow sand and coconut trees that looked as if they had been painted on a wide canvas. It was one of the loveliest anchorages we saw on the entire trip. We cooked supper ashore, the boys persuading Alice that study hall would not be necessary and trying to convince Spook they'd provide plenty of fish. Fortunately, he hedged the bet and brought food for supper. One boy finally speared one small fish.

Moving a few miles to Norman Island, we dropped anchor in a big U-shaped cove and had a fine time exploring. Some snorkeled and watched the thousands of tiny yellow, green, blue and red tropical fish swimming in large schools among the brightly colored sea fans and brain coral. While others explored the phosphorescent caves reputed to be those in Robert Louis Stevenson's *Treasure Island*, J.C. and a couple of the crew went ashore to hike to the ruins of an old plantation, became lost and didn't return until shortly before midnight. They had to follow the shoreline for hours, climbing over and around rocks and trees until they finally found our anchorage.

The Baths at Virgin Gorda was fun. Huge, smooth, water-worn boulders 60-80 feet high stand piled haphazardly at one end of the island, forming large underwater caverns and clear pools as the tides come and go beneath them. One can crawl, slip sideways and climb down into the caverns and walk through the clear salt pools by the dim light that filters through crevices in the boulders above. The Baths was a good spot for spearfishing, and we dined several times on fish speared there.

We moved on to the Dutch Island of Saba, a beautiful but forbidding place. It's not possible for a ship to anchor there because the island is the top of a volcanic cone and the drop from the land is sheer into hundreds of fathoms of water. The only landing is on a rocky shale area about a half-acre in size and one gets ashore by riding in native dories that surge through the heavy surf at full speed and land heavily upon the rocks.

One half of the crew remained on *Albatross* while the other visited the village of Bottom, reached after a long ride up a steep hill by jeep. This is a neat, clean, pretty collection of Dutch fishermen's cottages. The people I saw looked very much alike; Saba is isolated from most of the world, and its inhabitants marry and raise children amongst themselves. The men have reputations as fine fishermen and sailors.

Albatross was a dry ship as far as alcohol was concerned. The adults agreed it would be best not to bring beer or liquor aboard because many of the boys were very young. Except for the adults, the crew was not supposed to drink ashore, either, but one way or another, a few boys managed to imbibe pretty freely from port to port. A couple of them got high in Bermuda, but nothing much was said about it. Shortly after we sailed south, though, Skipper and Alice laid down some stiff penalties for drinking. Even so, some of the crew broke the rules at Saba and were caught in the act by Alice. It turned out that the rules were not very realistic ones (such as loss of shore privileges at our next port) because one of the main purposes of the trip was to give the boys opportunities to see and know different cultures and places. After one or two attempts at enforcement, we all realized we were defeating our own purposes. Some of the older boys had been allowed to drink moderately with their parents, and it didn't make much sense to try to change them. About the best we could do was find some compromise that wasn't harsh or unfair to the younger crew members.

The problem worked itself out in the end, and as we said and did less about drinking, the boys drank less and stopped thinking of it as if it were something important. It would have been a simpler situation if everyone on board had been a little older, but everyone was learning, Skipper and Alice included.

On warm evenings the crew slept on deck, rolled in blankets. The charthouse was a favorite spot, too, and sometimes it was like stumbling over an obstacle course of sleeping bodies to reach the log or to check a course on the chart. Several boys rigged up "penthouses" in the ship's longboats atop the galley, reading and sleeping there regularly.

At Nelson's Dockyard in Antigua we spent more than a week, and the group of tourists and natives who watched us lay alongside the quay must have thought we were a traveling comic opera. The anachronistic, circus-painted red-and-white *Albatross* always looked out of place everywhere we went, but at Nelson's Dockyard our crew helped promote the carnival image. Terry Blair was his usual hustling, scrambling self: one minute he was forward handling lines; the next he was aft telling the mate how to steer, then he shot below to the engine room (where he was supposed to be all the time) and bellowed up unintelligible commands to those on deck. I'm sure those who watched his performance from shore were convinced he was three people because he moved so fast to so many places.

Skipper stood on the charthouse shouting orders to the man at the wheel and to several of the crew who were trying to get lines ashore, while at the same time waving to the Nicholson brothers (old friends of the Sheldons) waiting on the quay. It was a frenetic time, not at all typical of our dockings, but we were all a bit excited about getting to Antigua. Most of us expected mail and film and other packages from home, and we all looked forward to several days of relaxation ashore exploring Lord Nelson's 18th-century Caribbean naval headquarters.

As it turned out, we saw more of the little landlocked dockyard basin and its historic buildings and ruins than we saw of the rest of Antigua. Skipper had work details all planned for most of us. *Albatross* was to be chipped, red-leaded, sanded, painted, varnished, careened and bottom painted, and that was just the beginning.

Things worked out better for me, J. C. and Spook than for the boys, however. Our job was more supervisory than physical, though it was time-consuming. We got away in the evenings, though, and went to town several times by taxi. I always had to be back in time to get some sleep before rousing the crew at 6:30 a.m. I was *Albatross'* unofficial Master at Arms and had to roll the boys out an hour before breakfast so they could make their bunks, clean the heads, wash down the decks and polish the ship's brass before classes began at 8:15.

Nelson's Dockyard turned out to be an interesting place. Besides the main buildings where we docked, there were numerous ruins in the hills around the area. Some had well-built stone arches still standing, and the crew scoured the countryside for minié balls, bayonets, belt buckles, uniform buttons and other artifacts and evidence of the battles fought there hundreds of years ago. Spook and I hiked up to the old military cemetery one afternoon, high above the harbor and saw a number of ancient cannon emplacements that once guarded the narrow opening through which all ships passed to enter the harbor.

Our best times in Antigua came one weekend when The Trinity rented a car and spent almost three days touring the island. Inadvertently we crashed a private party one night at the newly opened Jabberwock Club, where the famous Brute Force Steel Band was playing. It looked as though it were open for business with lots of cars parked around it and people entering. Once inside the lovely new club we found it had been reserved for the evening by an American contractor named Johnson for a big birthday bash for his daughter. The Nicholson brothers, who run a charter boat business at the Dockyard and a travel bureau in town, were present. One of them spotted my beard, sidled up behind me and said in a demanding voice: "What are you doing here?" I was embarrassed, but just for a moment. He smiled broadly when I turned to see who it was. He directed the three of us to the open bar where we soon began to catch up with other guests on frozen daiquiris.

Johnson had a delicious buffet supper laid out, and we consumed more than our share. Brute Force was in great form and played the best "pan" music I've ever heard. Later in the evening or early morning we had our picture taken with them.

Spook said the picture looked like a Swedish industrialist (me) trying to sell a new steel mill to an Arab politician (Spook) and his German banker (J.C.).

During the Jabberwock party we met a Mexican who managed the Mill Reef Club, a private haven for millionaires on the other side of Antigua. He and Spook carried on a long conversation in Spanish that ended in an invitation to visit the club the following Sunday.

Once there, we were entertained royally. We sipped cocktails in the beautiful bar, watched sailboats from the terrace overlooking the bay, drove around the private roads to see the large estates of some of the millionaires, took pictures of everything (including the home of playwright Archibald MacLeish), and ended at the private beach for a swim and more drinks. As we left, the manager told us apologetically that we could not return again until we were millionaires and had become members. I replied that we might not be back for a while.

I had arranged with friends at home to send regular shipments of film and cigars, and a large box of each awaited me in Antigua. Just before we left, Alice came aboard with them, one under each arm, escorted by two native guards in spotless white uniforms whose job it was to see that all goods in transit remained unopened until we sailed. Chuck's scuba gear came aboard in the same way; we felt very important to have so much attention paid to our mail.

We visited Les Saintes, two tiny French islands near Martinique, and Dominica, a large, high island where the last descendants of the primitive Carib Indians still live in the mountains. We had a real fright on the night we left Portsmouth harbor at Dominica, though. We hauled the anchor at midnight as the crew returned from a long day ashore, and everybody was tired and sleepy. With no wind, we throbbed along the towering, rocky coast under power. J.C. and I had the watch with Tom and Tod. Tod was at the wheel, and J.C. and I took a couple of deck chairs to the starboard side of the charthouse, propped our feet on the bulwarks and lighted cigars. *Albatross* was headed east, the sky was clear and full of stars, and we quickly picked out the Southern Cross, hanging like a diamond pendant high above.

Tom was posted forward as bow watch; we wanted to avoid the dozens of lobster traps and buoys that lay in the coastal waters along the island, and with the bright sky it was not hard to spot them. As J.C. and I talked and smoked, three-quarters of an hour passed quickly. I looked up to find the Southern Cross again, but it was no longer there. I asked J.C. if he could see it but he couldn't either. Glaring at each other, we had the same thought: sure enough, the Southern Cross was hanging directly off our stern. Dead ahead were the high, rocky cliffs of Dominica, the white surf pounding across a long reef and crashing up the shore. J.C. ran aft, found Tod fast asleep with his head on his arms, which were draped across the wheel. He shook him.

"What's your course?"

Tod awoke, belligerent. "I'm only off a couple of degrees. What's the fuss about?"

"Look ahead. You're off 90 degrees!"

Tod saw the breakers and straightened up. J.C. gave him an extra hour at the wheel, and we stood by him the whole time to make sure he was alert. Later, Tod confessed that he and Boot had enjoyed a romantic encounter in Portsmouth just before they returned to the ship that night and was in no condition to stand watch.

When things settled down, I went forward to talk to Tom, our bow watch.

"Did you notice we were headed for that reef?"

"Sure. I just figured Skipper wanted to get closer to shore," he calmly replied.

"How far in were you going to let us get before you said something?"

"I don't know. Nobody told me to say anything. I'm supposed to watch for lobster traps."

Tom's candor and innocence convinced me he really had seen nothing unusual about the situation. *Albatross* seemed to be a sturdy, dependable ship, and we all knew Skipper was an excellent navigator, so Tom's composure and lack of concern was natural enough at his age, especially given his little experience on a sailing ship. Only two or three of the crew had sailed before they boarded *Albatross*, but over the months they became more imaginative about the consequences of feeling too secure and too confident at sea. I made certain they all read Dana, Conrad and Melville in our English classes, and we covered Conrad's The Secret Sharer with special thoroughness. Some began to understand that when they felt most secure, that was the very moment when they were most vulnerable to disaster.

Albatross anchored a day at Carriacou, and we had a chance to watch native schooners loading and unloading cargoes at the small wharf. Everything from oil drums to people are transported on these schooners, and they are the chief form of transportation between the islands. Often their sails are made of whatever material is at hand, including varicolored flour sacks and cast-off pieces of khaki.

On a tour of St. Vincent, Spook and I had a garrulous cab driver who insisted on telling us the intimate details of his private life, including the recent death of his brother in a car accident. When we drove by the accident scene, he stopped the car, got out and explained with gestures just how and where his brother had been hit and the point at which the death car had finally stopped. Then, to Spook's delight and my dismay, he rolled on the ground and acted out every movement of his brother's death throes. Fortunately, the brother had not taken long to die; had the final act lasted very long, we would have attracted a fair-sized crowd. As it was, we received an inquisitive stare from the driver of a passing truck and the quiet, curious awe of three small children who had been playing in a yard nearby.

Back in the car, the driver continued to talk about the accident. To make his tale more interesting, he drove by the home of the man who had struck his brother and pointed out the damaged car parked by the road, making certain we saw the still-broken headlight and crumpled fender. When the owner of the car came out of the house, our driver greeted him cordially and proudly introduced us, proving, I suppose, that fame is where you find it, or that there is no accounting for taste.

The tour was a success despite the talkative driver. We saw our first black lava beach, soft and jet-black sand with foaming white surf rolling up on it. St. Vincent is a beautiful island of green farms, tiny villages and spectacular mountain scenery, but it's probably a good deal less-picturesque now than we found it in 1960. Our driver explained that a jet airport was being constructed and the island was preparing for an influx of visitors.

We amused the locals greatly, or at least my red beard did. Once, as we rounded a curve near some thatched huts by a stream where some women were washing clothes, one of them dropped her laundry on the rocks when she saw me leaning out the car window and threw both hands over her head, shouting, "Oh, God! Oh, God! What is it?" Spook said, "Well, Big Daddy, at least she knew your name."

A few miles from St. Vincent lies the tiny island of Bequia, one of my two or three favorites in the BWI. *Albatross* anchored in the deep, horseshoe-shaped harbor just 200 yards off the white beach. At least 30 other vessels were anchored about us, mostly the stubby, short-masted native schooners we had seen so many of in the Caribbean. Two or three were careened in low water along the beach for bottom painting, their hulls glistening in the hot sun.

Bequia's harbor is fringed with palms; and bananas, oranges, limes and other fruit that grow in abundance. In the evening Spook, J.C. and I visited the Sunny Caribbee hotel on the harbor side, for dinner. One evening as we sat quietly on the big porch there enjoying a rum collins and the sunset, the bartender sadly announced he was out of limes and could not make more drinks for us. Though a near-catastrophe, Spook averted it. A bit hard of hearing as a result of a childhood illness, he'd missed the bitter news, but I relayed it to him with appropriate melancholy expressions.

Spook leaped to his feet and shouted "Voila!" Plunging a hand into the canvas bag he often carried, he brought forth a bounty of large, fresh limes he had picked a few hours earlier. Our tall, black bartender accepted them with a wry smile and proceeded to build our drinks. The crisis was over.

Spook relaxed visibly in his big rocking chair, saying, "Big Daddy, I live for moments like this."

I recall many occasions that enchanted Spook and made his every day a gift. He experienced a level of *joie de vivre* that I have seen in only one or two others. His was a gentle, sensitive, curious approach to the world, and almost everyone he met responded in kind.

On one occasion, while walking with him along a dusty path in the back country of Martinique, we passed some small children carrying fruit and flowers they had just picked. When Spook smiled and bowed, one of the little girls approached him shyly and offered a bouquet and some fruit, which he gallantly accepted. The little girl was delighted, and her heart went out to Spook. Reluctantly she rejoined her comrades, and together they went off down the path, looking back and waving. Children especially recognized Spook's love of life and considered him a kindred spirit.

One night the three of us sat on deck listening to the faint rustling of palm trees along the shore. The night was black, and we could not see any of the ships anchored near us. I could almost feel the darkness, as if it had texture and weight pressing down from the hills surrounding the harbor. If we looked hard, we could see a tiny star or two glowing faintly through a thin mist that gave each star its own halo. The darkness and the mist enveloped us and quieted our voices, and we could not see each other though we were only a few feet apart.

J.C. flipped a cigarette butt over the side; it hissed as it fell on the water. I thought I heard something alongside the ship and peered over the bulwarks, but it was only one of our longboats gently thumping the hull. Then I saw a quick spurt of orange-red fire from across the water near where the shore would be if I could see it. It flickered, then became a flame. Another orange flash, then two or three at once. Other flames appeared until there was a cluster of them flaring orange-red above the black water, with a narrow path of yellow light extending across the bay from each flame to *Albatross*. Each yellow path seemed strewn with flashing golden leaves and ran through the dark forest of spars and rigging dimly silhouetted by the strange, flickering lights.

The lights were torches held high above the water by fishermen. We sat motionless and fascinated as they bobbed steadily and slowly toward us. Each torch was held aloft by a fisherman in the bow of a small, double-end boat; a second one rowed. Each boat with its two fishermen was a thing apart from all the others, each a vivid orange picture floating through the mist and darkness of the night.

The torchbearers held their torches high above their heads, leaned as far out over the water as they dared and swept a small, short-handled net silently and rhythmically through the water. They were bait fishing. The light attracted small fish to the bow of the boat, and the net handler dipped his net softly into the water. Each time the net entered the water, it caught a few small silver fish held in the net by centrifugal force as the net moved constantly through its full circle over the fisherman's head and down again into the water.

The boats glided silently through the harbor and made no wake. As the nets were lifted high and descended to the black water, they trailed drops of flashing orange light. We did not speak or move but watched intently, enchanted by the mystery. One by one, the torches burned out and the fishermen beached their tiny boats. The mist and darkness closed upon us, and we sat without talking for a long while.

J.C. went to bed. Spook said, "They seemed so good at it, Big Daddy."

"I know. Yes, it was natural, and something they've been doing for a very long time."

"They probably learned how from their fathers. I'll bet

they catch bait the same way it's been done for hundreds of years," Spook said.

"It's nice to think that something as old as that still works, isn't it?"

Spook did not answer right away but thought for a while. "You know," he said slowly, "they didn't know they were impressing us. They didn't know we were here. They didn't care about that. They were just doing what they had to do to stay alive. And that's what made it beautiful. It was real. It was so real."

As usual, Spook had gotten to the heart of the experience. I always looked forward to his comments, whether about a book we had both read, someone we had met or an experience we had shared. Spook called our discussions "building an elephant," after the mythological blind men who had each touched a different part of the elephant and described it in terms of his own needs and imagination.

Spook and I built many elephants on *Albatross.*

The Caribbean is a photographer's paradise. All the colors are deep and rich, and every street corner and beach present a hundred opportunities. Skies are clear, blue and high, and clouds take on shapes that confuse the imagination. Plants shine green and yellow and red. Sunsets and sunrises are beautiful beyond description, and one wants to photograph everything every day — boats with multicolored sails, gaudy taxis and buses, houses painted blue, pink, white, green, yellow, red. Everybody has a garden full of flowers splotched with every color you can name.

I didn't have a camera when I signed on *Albatross* so I purchased an inexpensive Japanese 35 mm. It turned out to be one of the best buys I ever made. I shot more than 3,000 color frames with it, a lifetime of use for the average camera owner, and it held together until just a few days before the untimely end of the voyage.

When I no longer carried the camera, I was surprised to feel relieved of an onerous burden because I had become so concerned with taking pictures most of the time. I was serving the camera instead of it serving me. I'd missed much of the full involvement with people and places because I was running to get the camera or framing pictures instead of relaxing and enjoying what went on. I decided that if I ever made another trip, history would not repeat itself.

Of course I'm glad I have the pictures (they're my only record of the voyage now); I lost about 500 I had taken of the Yucatan and the San Blas Indians, but those I sent home from port to port were a good visual record of most of the cruise. Yet I'd swap them all for my journal, more than 50,000 words of reflections, sketches and descriptions.

One sunny day, *Albatross* anchored off the coastal village of St. Pierre, Martinique, and we lowered a longboat to go ashore. An attractive little place, we strolled around it for hours, visiting the museum dedicated to the memory of the 45,000 inhabitants who died in the gigantic eruption of Mt. Pelée, the now-dormant volcano that looms over the western end of the town. Only one man, in a dungeon, survived the great shower of ash and molten rock that cascaded down upon the population in 1902.

The little goateed museum curator happily showed us around, demonstrating light bulbs that still worked though the disaster had happened nearly 60 years before. He proudly pointed out the names of celebrities who had visited his museum and quickly spun the register around when we signed our names to see if any of us were famous. He seemed disappointed when he discovered that we weren't movie stars, renowned writers or political figures.

Farther along the coast of Martinique we anchored in the wide bay before the big city of Fort de France and remained there for four or five days. The Unholy Trinity enjoyed excellent French cookery, and it was pleasant to walk in the big park near the waterfront. I also learned the difference between the French terms for "raw" and "rare." One evening we ordered a fine *vin ordinaire blanc* and settled back to anticipate our food. When the entree was served, I reached across the table to put my cigar into an ash tray when suddenly

Spook let out a cackling laugh and pointed to the dish before me. I had been served a large mound of cold, raw ground beef with a raw egg in the half-shell sitting on top.

Trying to keep a straight face, Spook insisted I should eat it to avoid embarrassing the waitress, but when I looked up at her, she was doing her best to keep from laughing. She wasn't sure what was wrong, but she understood that the joke (whatever it was) was on me. After much frustrated discussion in my very broken French, I conveyed to her that I wanted the dish cooked. When I lifted the plate and held a lighted match beneath it, she got the idea immediately, took the plate and ran to the kitchen, laughing all the way. Spook and J.C. were no help; they both spoke French much better than I but were not about to rescue me. I think they knew all along what was going to happen as soon as I ordered.

J.C. did help me haggle in the Fort de France marketplace, though. I wanted a wide straw hat to add to the collection I had been building from port to port. The market, one of the largest and most colorful in the Caribbean, was about a square block in size and covered with a tin roof and skylights. Vendors sat or stood at hundreds of stalls and in the middle of the floor selling fish, meats, candies, fruit, vegetables, hats, dresses and all kinds of five-and-dime ware. For a few francs J.C. procured the hat I wanted, but I'm sure the woman we bought it from felt she had gotten the best of us. And she probably had.

Castries on the island of St. Lucia is a relatively new city full of freshly painted houses neatly arranged in a city-block system, unlike the typical Caribbean town with twisting, rambling lanes and haphazard system of roads. Castries suffered a fire in the late 1940s, and much of its downtown section was destroyed. The British helped rebuild it, and today it is a modern, bustling port with many tourist vessels and freighters calling there regularly.

Albatross had its troubles in Castries. We had been warned about thieves and to keep a close watch on the ship. To avoid the need to post night watches, Skipper moved the ship out into the bay after two nights alongside the quay.

Tod and Terry stirred things up by bringing aboard a "lady of the evening" one night. My bunk was just under the galley, and I was awakened around midnight by unusual noises on deck, excited whisperings and a good deal of scurrying around, so I went topside to see what was going on. Tod was taking a bucket bath alongside the galley, and as soon as he saw me, he hastened to explain that he was responsible for the noise and had only wanted to cool off. It was a hot night and all seemed quiet, so I returned below and got back to sleep.

Next day I noticed several of the crew in small groups talking very mysteriously. I knew something was going on but I didn't know what until a hint or two was dropped by Spook, who had evidently been taken into confidence about the previous night's visitor. I didn't know what to do. I had no facts or first-hand information, so I waited to see what came of the business.

I don't suppose it's possible for young boys to keep such a secret very long, especially aboard a ship where they live under close conditions. A day or so later, Alice approached as I was sitting on deck and asked what I knew. She was certain that both Tod and Terry were involved and that Terry had swapped a couple of his white dress shirts for the lady's favors, a detail I had heard nothing about.

She finally got the whole story, a sordid and dangerous business, and Alice and Skipper were justifiably upset. The safety of the crew was a large responsibility, and for a couple of boys to bring a woman aboard was to expose the whole crew not only to disease but to the possibility of serious physical danger from the wharf thieves. Alice handled it as well as anyone could; she ordered Tod and Terry into her cabin to submit to an old-fashioned "short-arm" medical inspection. They were terribly embarrassed, of course, and became the butt of jokes for weeks thereafter. Both were restricted to the ship for the next few ports and suffered by missing some pleasant excursions ashore.

J.C. and I thought it might be a good time to have a

serious discussion with Skipper and Alice about several matters relating to classes. We'd completed a series of semester exams just the week before, and only three boys had passed all of their classes satisfactorily. Most had failed two or more subjects, and half had failed every one. J.C. and I felt that schoolwork had become a secondary feature of the voyage, and we wanted to get things back into what we thought was proper perspective.

The necessity of keeping to a schedule of ports often caused Skipper to haul the anchor, start the diesel and move on even while J.C. and I were trying to teach. No teacher can compete with sail handling and shouted commands, particularly when one or two students are suddenly ordered on deck to stand watch before the class is over. We felt too much was expected of the boys, that few had understood they would do so much hard labor maintaining *Albatross*.

It was a defeating business. The boys lost interest in everything except finding new ways to avoid studying. They grew sloppy and dirty in personal appearance, their bunks looked like rag bins, they came to meals straight from sanding and painting or from the engine room, and made infrequent attempts to wash before eating or going to bed.

One or two still tried. Schoolwork was easy for them, so the voyage was a rewarding experience and they were relaxed, secure and good-natured. However, after five months aboard, the ship's company showed more scowls than smiles.

The four adults had a long, private discussion in Skipper's cabin. Alice suggested we send Tod and Terry home before either caused more trouble. J.C. and I also thought it best for the ship if both went home, but Skipper was inclined to get rid of Terry and keep Tod. He was under some pressure regarding Tod since he knew Tod's father and had encouraged him to let his son come on the cruise. A few days later, Skipper told us that both boys would stay aboard, and that was the end of it until we reached Panama.

For about a week following the conference matters improved somewhat. The boys washed more often, picked up after themselves, changed their bed linen occasionally and were a little more cooperative about morning chores. Still, classes were a large, shared joke. They sat, paid no attention, studied little, and the night study period was rarely observed.

My sympathies were with them. Instead of trying to teach a full year of classes, it would have been far better to teach only navigation and biology (Skipper's and Alice's courses) and invest the salaries of the English and math teachers into hiring three full-time mates to head the watches and do some of the heavier labor aboard ship.

I'm sure Skipper and Alice would have done differently if they'd had the chance to start over and I believe a subsequent Ocean Academy voyage would have been more pleasant. Even so, at their request, J.C. and I prepared a list of recommendations concerning living conditions, school work, maintenance, personnel, etc.

Castries put on a good show for us on St. Lucia Day, and it was a colorful and exciting time. There were games and contests and dancing in the streets, steel bands on every corner, greased poles to climb and pigs to chase. Flags and ribbons flew from every house, rum casks were set up along the wharves and sidewalks, brightly colored costumes and long parades were everywhere, not to mention swimming and sailing races in the bay. Numerous sailing vessels arrived early in the morning with loads of visitors from nearby islands, and our ship's crew had the day off to join the festivities.

Spook, J.C. and I attended a big dance that night to watch the show staged by dozens of amateur performers. Spook joined in and put on a performance himself. He was a comic sight to see, shuffling and flopping around the floor, trying to keep in step with the locals, who changed the beat every few minutes. Two fellows kept bringing me rum from a big barrel at one end of the long room and would not hear of my buying some for them. (Spook later explained they thought I was the skipper of *Albatross* because I was the only one aboard with a beard. In other ports the same thing happened, and recognizing a good thing when I saw it, I refused to disillusion any of my kind hosts.)

A group of musicians had set up their steel drums in the center of town, and we could hear faint shouts and melodies wafting through the open windows of the dance hall. Some of the crowd drifted off toward the new music and we followed. They were conducting what's called a "clash," or a battle of the bands.

A large sign painted in crooked letters on a bedsheet proclaimed the name of one group to be Lord Dynamite and his Savage Sharks. A hundred feet farther down the street were The Devil's Minions. Soon we learned that dynamite was stronger than the devil, and the former was awarded the prize — five gallons of black rum that were immediately shared with all the bands and any bystanders near enough to grab a jug as it passed from hand to hand. None of these bands could match the virtuosity of Brute Force, whom we had heard in Antigua, though.

Just a few miles from Castries lies tiny Pigeon Island. A grand old lady named Miss Josett Legh reigned supreme there, having gathered a group of interesting people to enjoy the island with her. She rented cottages to painters, retired scientists, writers, etc. and served delicious dinners in a grass-roofed house on the beach. Crayfish abound in the surrounding shallow waters, and dinner at her tropical club was wonderful. One could consume all the seafood or chicken and white wine desired for just a dollar.

The Trinity dined there twice, with Skipper and Alice along one night, and everyone seated on comfortable rattan chairs in our bare feet and shorts. Suddenly Skipper jumped up, knocked over his chair and let out a big "Yow!" A large rat scurried across the floor. Skipper shouted, "The damned thing bit my toe!" Alice took it calmly, saying, "I hope the rat doesn't get sick."

Miss Legh explained with a smile that she had lots of rats around, pointing to several taking their ease in the rafters above us. She looked upon them as company, I think, and was quite satisfied with their presence. It was all part of the atmosphere at Pigeon Island.

I had my first taste of whale meat at Pigeon Island. Alice bought large whale steaks at Castries from a fisherman, and Spook cut them up and fried them. It was like tough, salty beef with almost no fishy taste. Later, Spook ground the leftovers, mixed in some chopped onions and made some very good whaleburgers. Before leaving, we speared several dozen crayfish on the nearby reef, explored the ruins of an old fort and a crumbling house and had many fascinating talks with Miss Legh and her guests.

Our crew fought a forest fire, too. It began as a small trash fire that had been put out, or so Miss Legh thought, but the wind fanned it later. The boys extinguished it after a two-hour battle, using buckets, brooms, blankets and shovels from the ship. They became heroes of Pigeon Island, and Miss Legh treated the firefighters to cold refreshments.

This casual, beautiful spot was hard to leave. Tall palms lined the soft, white beach, and the green island rose steeply behind the clubhouse. No one hurried, fruit and fish were both plentiful and free for the taking, and the warm, sunny days and sparkling nights combined to make Pigeon Island unique and refreshing.

When we fetched Grenada, I knew we were near because I could smell it. Grenada is called the spice island of the West Indies, and in the soft, warm air around *Albatross* hung the scent of cinnamon, nutmeg, ginger, clove and mace. Skipper stood in the foretop watching for a marker, calling down "Port a point." The helmsman swung the wheel, repeating the order, to confirm it. He found his marker and brought *Albatross* to the mouth of Grenada's large harbor. The way ahead opened up into a horseshoe-shaped bay, and we sailed in silently.

The crew furled the jibs and then the staysails, the boys working automatically and quietly from long hours of practice. "Drop the main," called Skipper from the foretop, and a minute later we heard , "Ready with the anchor — let her go!" With a jangling of chain it struck the water and went home.

Albatross lay to in a lovely harbor surrounded by soft yellow lights that twinkled along the curving quay. The clicking of palms high in the hills above us and the gentle lapping of tiny waves along the hull were all that existed to remind us that we were still awake and not in a dream. From shore came the slow, quiet strum of a guitar. A huge full moon rose gradually over the hills behind the sleeping town and silhouetted the spars of other ships at anchor. Our white hull and masts must have looked strange as we sat motionless. Had anyone seen us enter, he might have mistaken us for a ghost ship, a reminder of times long gone.

Next morning the scene was far different. Cars and people filled the road extending around the harbor. Shops opened, boys on bicycles peddled vigorously up the steep hill that led to the main part of town, gulls hoping for a handout flew above.

After morning classes and lunch, Alice set off to shop, returning with a whole hog that Spook expertly butchered and stored in the deep-freeze. She brought a half-dozen spices, too. Spook had been looking forward to this port to replenish his stocks, and the best in the world can be had there.

That afternoon we put *Albatross'* stern to the quay and held her off with a bow anchor. J.C. and I walked into town, with Spook joining us later at a pub.

The road around the harbor was under repair, and we noticed a dozen women carrying dirt on small square boards balanced on their heads. They worked in two lines like a bucket brigade, one line moving to where the dirt was dumped and the other returning to the truck for more. A foreman stood nearby, and I asked him about the project: "Why not just run the truck over there and dump all the dirt at once? With a bulldozer you could lay the whole road in half a day."

He looked at me stiffly, then realized I was not trying to be smart but simply didn't understand his method of road building. He smiled, white teeth flashing and one arm gesturing toward the women.

"My way feed a dozen families, sir. Your way make

them all go hungry."

His logic was irrefutable. I thought about it as we walked to town, beginning to understand why in so many undeveloped areas that the Western system had proved unworkable: "Your way make them all go hungry."

We visited a rum distillery and sampled its product, drawing directly from 500-gallon casks. If one brought his own jug, the dark, delicious brew cost just 75 cents per gallon. Because we couldn't take it aboard ship, we had to be content with what we could carry within.

We made considerable use of the buses with imaginative names instead of numbers, such as "Baby Smile," "The Road Buster," "Father Time" and "Hell's Doors." Each was painted according to a color scheme devised by its owner, and when several buses are seen together in a town square they presented a visual chaos.

The Trinity rode inland to see a huge arrowroot plant, stopping along the way to watch the harvesting of cocoa. Heaps of the bright yellow gourd-like pods were piled around the countryside in deep green grass. At a waterfall we stopped, stripped, and plunged into a cool, clear pool for a swim.

The relative civilization of Grenada contrasted sharply with the solitude and tranquillity of the tiny Tobago Islands. These dozens of tiny islets are perfect gems of tropical beaches and tiny coves. Each seemed to have a curving white beach with long palms hanging over it and a high hill rising above. Mostly coral, they dotted the horizon as far as one could see, and the beautiful waters are alive with brilliantly colored tropical fish and other forms of sea life. Beneath our hull were acres of undulating red, blue and green sea fans and huge, white brain coral.

It was a quiet, restful place and perfect for celebrating Christmas. With decorations provided by Alice, the crew festooned the main cabin with crepe paper, tinsel and silvery baubles. Spook cooked two turkeys with all the trimmings plus other traditional Christmas foods. The boys opened their Christmas boxes from home and exchanged small gifts with ᴏᴛher. Skipper and Alice held a short Christmas service on deck beneath a star-bright sky. Carols seemed incongruous in such tropical surroundings, but the boys sang lustily. Later, Spook brought up kettles of fresh popcorn, and the crew ate their fill while describing past Christmases at home.

Albatross visited the big city of Port of Spain, Trinidad, but during our three days there the crew made only brief visits. Skipper had anchored a mile or so away from the wharves, so it was no simple matter to get ashore. Spook, J.C. and I spent an interesting day visiting the expansive horticultural gardens and parks full of orchids, cinnamon trees, and hundreds of varieties of plants and flowers.

Port of Spain is a real metropolis of streets full of people of different nationalities and countless stores and restaurants. We had a fine night at a local calypso club, where we spent half the time declining offers of friendship from a dozen or so pretty ladies headquartered there. It was an evening of delicious food, fire and limbo dancers, singers and comics. When it was time to sing a rousing version of "The Big Bamboo," we were included in several impromptu verses to the great delight of some of *Albatross'* crew.

I added to my growing collection of artifacts by acquiring an Indian sword cane and a turban. Stowage in my bunk was getting scarce, but I found it hard to resist some of the beautifully handmade canes and hats. Spook wryly observed that I might do better to collect stamps, but canes and hats appealed to my suppressed desire for fancy costume. I searched everywhere for a silver-headed cane to go with the gentleman's evening cape I had found in Fort de France but with no luck. It's just as well. Stalking my university campus in an outfit such as that might have become grounds for a sanity hearing. In St. Vincent I bought a long, white shark's-vertebrae cane, and I'm certain that it alone would have caused more than enough comment, had I been able to get it home. At Willemstad on Curaçao in the Netherlands West Indies I found a very heavy and handsome black mahogany cane and a high, black bowler, "the perfect ensemble for attending a state funeral," J.C. commented.

We were in Curaçao for more than 10 days. A modern city, Willemstad offered free-port prices and several excellent restaurants for *Albatross*' sea-weary crew. A group of pretty blond young ladies from Peter Stuyvesant College took the crew in hand and invited them to parties, dances, ball games and tours of the island. The boys returned the kindnesses by inviting them to a day-sail on *Albatross*. They accepted eagerly and came aboard at 8 a.m.

We moved up the harbor under power, then set sails and came grandly down past the city and out through Queen Emma, the swinging pontoon bridge, to the delight of hundreds of people on shore who had not seen such a large sailing ship in a long time. The girls became terribly seasick but recovered during the afternoon and had a fine time of it.

Albatross lay alongside the main waterfront street in Willemstad, and every day large tankers and passenger liners passed us. There were at least 20 big ships in any 24-hour period, most of them bringing crude oil to Shell from Venezuela just 30 miles away. In the early morning dozens of small boats sailed by on the way to the famous floating market, where perhaps 50 boats at a time rafted to sell their cargoes of Venezuelan fruits and vegetables.

Curaçao is an island without a natural source of fresh water; all of it is made from the sea in a large evaporation plant near Willemstad. This made hot showers hard to come by. I walked across Queen Emma's bridge to the opposite side of the harbor, rented a room at the local YMCA and arranged with the management to let all our crew use the shower. Most took advantage of a chance to get clean, and there was a constant stream of boys all afternoon.

One experience in Curaçao I shall never forget. Through a mutual friend in the United States I met Dr. George Hopkins, a longtime resident physician in Willemstad and much respected. He asked one day if I should like to see Campo Alegre. I had no idea what it was, so he explained, "So much sea traffic here brought us many prostitutes who roamed the town day and night. There were drunken sailors in the streets, fights and much venereal disease. We decided to do something about it." The doctor's description was almost too pat; undoubtedly he had told the story dozens of times. "We knew we couldn't get rid of the prostitutes completely so we set aside a large area about six miles out of town and passed laws that required all prostitutes to live there. They can visit town during the day but must return to the compound at night. Now we are in control. The women are medically examined weekly and must keep their clearance certificates up to date. It's all very organized now, and we have no more trouble in town."

In his 70s, Dr. Hopkins was obviously proud of the solution to Curaçao's social problem. I accepted his invitation, and he called ahead to make arrangements for our visit. J.C., Skipper and I went out: Spook had a date that night and couldn't come along.

Campo Alegre was not, as its name implied, a place of happiness. We took a taxi, all of us apprehensive but making much small talk to hide our reservations. The driver stopped before a large gate. The whole area, perhaps a half-mile square, was surrounded by an eight-foot barbed-wire fence; the only entrance and exit was past several uniformed guards. We were searched for weapons and cameras, then directed to a wide, unpainted building that served as a canteen, saloon, and restaurant. On the porch of the building were three or four of the women wearing cheap evening gowns or tight, black satin pants. It was a hot night and all the girls were sweating through their clothing as they sat or stood with two or three sailors drinking beer. We entered the saloon and sat at a table, very conscious of the fact that we were out of place.

The plain wooden floor was dirty and littered with bottle caps, bits of paper and candy wrappers. We ordered beer and talked with animation about nothing, trying to pretend we were not really interested in where we were and that we were old hands in the whorehouses of the world.

One women approached us, about 50, wearing long, gray hair in a knot behind her head and a checkered shirt that hung loosely around her large hips. J.C. invited her to sit down. She told her appalling story, which we thought at first to be exaggerated and well rehearsed, but by the time we left the compound, we were all convinced she spoke the truth.

"I come from Panama," she said. "I have two small daughters there and I support them. We stay in each camp six weeks — the one in Mexico is next for me — then I can go to the camp in Panama for six weeks and see my daughters."

(Dr. Hopkins said the women were not allowed to stay in Curaçao and become citizens. The whole operation was international, highly organized like a traveling carnival with a regular stay in each country on the circuit.)

"Each week I pay the rent on my house here. I must buy my food at the compound restaurant every day, and there is not much money left over." What little she managed to save went home to her children in Panama.

"Would you like a beer?" I asked.

"Why don't you give me the money? It will buy my breakfast."

Her round, sweating face was perfectly serious. I gave her a half-dollar which she knotted tightly in a damp, dirty handkerchief she pulled from her brassiere. "I must be careful; the young girls steal," she said.

The three of us moved outside to a patio. A big gray rat hustled away beneath a scrubby bush, and large roaches scampered in every direction, avoiding our feet. A very pretty, heavily made-up young girl approached, and smiled, showing three gold teeth. She asked in Spanish if I would like her for the night; Skipper interpreted. He told her we were just visitors and did not want to use any woman. She scowled, spat at Skipper and cursed us loudly. It was a justifiable reaction under the circumstances. We felt ashamed of ourselves for looking at the women as if they were sociological case studies. There was nothing in it for them. We had no business being there.

We walked along the gravel road between the two rows of "houses." Each prostitute had her own two-room unpainted cottage; she lived in the back and attended to business in front. The tiny cottages were lit by candles; through the open door of each cottage we saw the image of the Virgin and a cross hanging on the wall. Some of the women sat on their front porches while others walked the sandy roads between the houses looking for customers. There were at least a hundred cottages inside the compound, most of them occupied and lighted. There were not many customers.

The women called to us as we walked along. Some hooted, some smiled, some lifted their skirts provocatively. One very proudly reeled off a list of unusual acts she was prepared to perform if we would favor her house.

I had seen enough of Campo Alegre. Skipper and J.C. agreed immediately when I suggested we return to our taxi. We had much less to say on the ride back than we had on the ride out. On the following night Spook returned to Campo Alegre. He was more honest and less self-conscious about the world than the other adults on *Albatross*. He enjoyed the women, and no doubt they enjoyed him, too.

Skipper Sheldon & Alice Sheldon M.D.

Spook

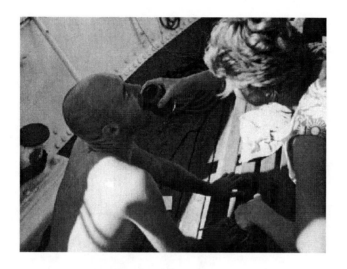

JC & Alice Sheldon

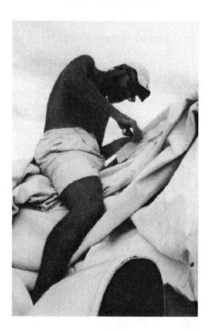

Big Daddy

Big Daddy's freshman college English class.
Clockwise - Tad, Robin, John, Chuck and Chris.

Big Daddy & Alice Sheldon M. D.

Mike and Skipper

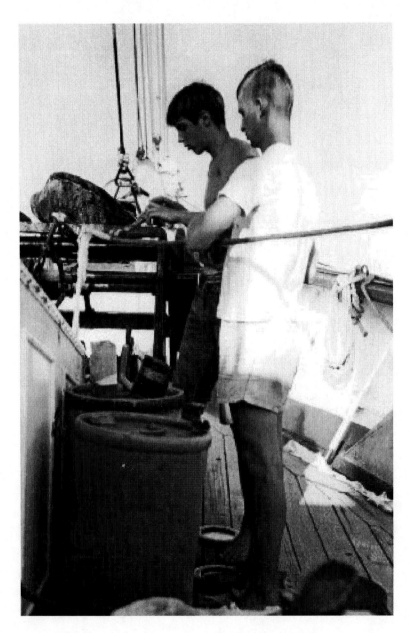

First Mate Bill and Tad

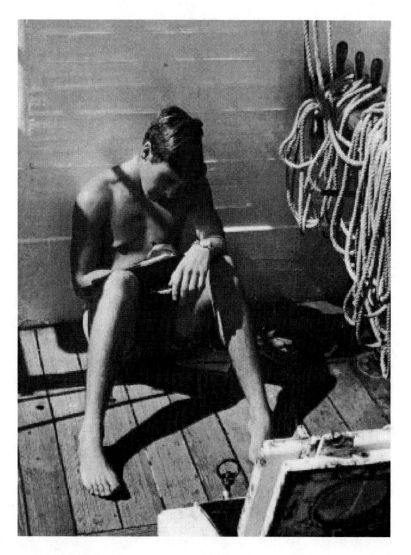

Bob

Chris and Chuck

Dick

Mate John

Phil and Rick

Phil

Rick and Tod

Robin (using the gaff)

Tim

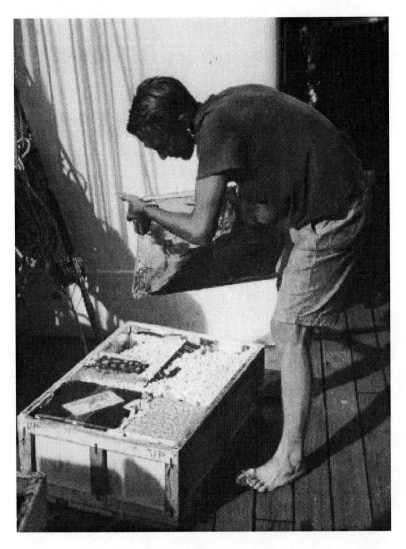

Tom

chapter four
CENTRAL AMERICA

The 10-day sail to Panama was one of the best we had during the voyage. We left the lush islands of the Caribbean with a 15-knot following breeze, and we had the trade winds all the way. We needed two boys at the wheel on every watch to keep the ship from broaching, and with most of our 5000 square feet of canvas flying, *Albatross* charged through the water as if alive. Everyone was in good spirits and settled quickly into regular watch routines. We caught plenty of dolphin and tuna, and Spook tried out new recipes he'd picked up in Willemstad. Gulls followed us for a day or two;

occasionally one dived for a silver lure at the end of a fishing line and became hooked. Immediately he would be brought aboard, carefully freed and set upon the stern rail. After much blinking and rustling of feathers he'd take to the air again.

Spook changed his appearance frequently. Once he let his black hair grow nearly to his shoulders, then suddenly appeared on deck with his head shaved. He'd grow a thick, dark beard, then shave it off except for a bristly mustache. Next he let the mustache grow into a wide handlebar waxed to thin points at the ends. He had native clothes he had bought all over the world, and once in a while he'd cook supper in a grass skirt. Occasionally he stalked the deck in a Roman toga, shouting to his galley slaves to bring more beans up from the lockers.

He did have his moods, though. Sometimes he did not respond to even a "good morning." Other times he might chase his help from the galley with a huge carving knife, laughing and cursing in Spanish.

Many of the boys did not understand these shifts, and that's exactly the way he wanted it. "I don't want anybody to wrap me up in a package and file me away in a drawer, Big Daddy," he'd say. "I don't want anybody taking me for granted." Thus he worked at retaining his individuality and took us off guard every chance he got.

Spook was proud of his cooking and sometimes bought food for the ship that Alice had not ordered so he could try something new or improve the menu. When the governor of Bermuda came aboard for lunch, Spook went out and bought fresh vegetables and fruits to serve, though he had been told to cook the usual fare. "I have my pride, after all," he protested. We missed Spook terribly when he had a day off and Alice took over the cooking.

Albatross dropped anchor at the entrance to the Panama Canal late one afternoon. The Trinity rowed ashore to Colon in the dinghy that evening to shower at the YMCA and have dinner in town. Early next morning our pilot boarded wearing the bright red baseball cap that identifies them, and we hoisted anchor and moved slowly under power toward the first lock.

Passing through the big canal was a new experience for most of us. It took a few minutes to become accustomed to the pilot's commands; he gave us our course in degrees, not in compass points to which we had become accustomed. I rode in the foretop most of the way as soon as my trick at the wheel was over. I had a marvelous view from up there, though as we locked up to Gatun Lake, I was sometimes below the tops of the locks because they were so deep.

The crew washed clothes in the fresh water of the lake, took deck baths, and Spook served lunch on deck for all hands so no one would miss any part of the passage. Eight hours after we started, we tied up in Balboa in the American Zone. Next day, *Albatross* took on supplies for the eight or nine weeks we would be in the Pacific cruising the Galapagos Islands.

Panama was fun for the whole crew. We had several days there and went to town frequently after morning classes. I bought a new cane and two handsome Panama hats, and J.C., Spook and I had good times at the Panama Hilton at the roulette wheel, where I picked up enough money to buy a tripod and wide-angle lens for my camera. Spook and I walked the streets of old Panama City, but Americans were not very welcome there. In one cafe we were asked to speak only Spanish, so we did. In one store I lusted after a Guatemalan shirt (a beautiful, intricately woven and patterned affair) but did not want to spend $40 for it. When I complained about the cost, the saleslady murmured something in Spanish that I did not understand. Spook interpreted.

"Big Daddy, she says it's six months of the work of a poor village woman."

Ashamed, I bought the shirt at its cover price.

We loaded *Albatross* with boxes of canned goods, dry cereals, extra canvas and lines, coils of rope, paint, a dozen drums of diesel fuel. It took hours to sort out and find space for all of it. The 21-foot tide at Balboa made things harder; one load might arrive when the ship's deck was level with the wharf, and the next would have to be lowered aboard from high above us.

We'd have to conserve water on the Galapagos trip. Skipper said he'd close all water valves on the way to and from the islands, and the crew would have to wash and brush their teeth in saltwater. Saltwater would be used in the galley for cooking and dishwashing, too. I filled two plastic five-gallon jugs with fresh water at Balboa so I could take sponge baths; with careful management, the 10 gallons would last until we returned to Panama. As it turned out, diesel fuel and fresh water were available in the Galapagos Islands, but in limited amounts and at very high prices.

Terry had become more of a problem than ever. His disinterest in school work, argumentativeness and physical dirtiness all caused dissension. The voyage was doing the boy no good, and his presence upset shipboard routines. Tod wasn't out of the woods, either, and was about as much trouble as Terry, though he was more experienced in dealing with people and better able to ingratiate himself with Skipper and Alice.

Another conference was held in the aft cabin, and the upshot was that Terry would go home. He was packed off on a plane, and Skipper arranged to have a security agent meet him at the airport in Mexico City, Terry's transfer point.

Everybody experienced pangs of guilt about Terry. The adults had failed to help a very insecure young boy, and the rest of the crew nearly ostracized him from the day he boarded. No one felt good about sending him home, but we all had to admit that *Albatross* was quieter and more pleasant without him.

Skipper and Alice finally understood what J.C. and I had recommended months before: that each boy be an A or B student at least 16 years old, from a decent home, and want very much to go on the cruise. Ocean Academy Ltd. hadn't received many applications for the first voyage and was obliged to take most of those who applied. J.C. and I felt that any future school voyage would be an improvement over the first.

I queried magazine editors, and one asked for submissions, one to be an article by the boys, describing their social life from port to port. Tim and Mike did a good job of it and got quite a kick out of suddenly becoming magazine writers.

I set aside one section of my journal for a list of differences between life ashore and at sea.

Motion was the basis for many of the differences. At sea, one is never completely still and must learn to sleep while bracing his body in his bunk. Also, one must eat in rhythm with the roll and pitch of the ship or risk missing his mouth with his fork. At sea one walks slowly and carefully, placing a foot when and where the ship allows, which is not always where he expects to place it. One learns to move in a bent position belowdecks to avoid banging his head on protruding objects, and to think about a move and its consequences before making it. None of this caution is necessary on land.

On a ship one learns a new language quickly. If he does not, he will be confused and something of a danger to his shipmates and will not fully enjoy his voyage. Brushing one's teeth and climbing aloft must conform to conditions. One cannot simply choose to eat, sleep, dress, start or stop an engine, put up or take down a sail, without considering the weather, the tides, the currents and the winds.

The ship, not the individual, is primary. One learns to serve the ship, anticipate her needs and fulfill them constantly. If he does not, the ship will not serve him. A ship has no highways or traffic signals to make her progress easy. At the mercy of the crew and the indifferent, uncaring seas, she sails under elemental conditions laid down by nature.

At sea one lives in a world of few people and the same scenes repeated day after day. Strong affections and stronger animosities can develop quickly. Personal habits of dress, speech and manner that could be ignored on land cannot be ignored on a ship. A ship makes a man tolerant or it drives him mad.

For its crew, the ship becomes the entire world. International affairs are inconsequential. The evening meal, the book one reads, the chair he wants to sit on, the condition of the heads, the length of his fingernails, the itch between his toes — these and a hundred other commonplaces become absurdly significant.

At sea there exist no stores, no markets, no repair shops. One learns to mend and make do or do without. Constant preparation is required, preparation for wind, rain, fog, sun, stormy seas. One never lets down his guard except at his own peril. A ship and her crew are most exposed to danger when her crew feels most secure. Even at anchor, a ship is vulnerable to the careless acts of her crew, the tides and currents.

chapter five
THE ENCANTADAS

On the run from Balboa to the Galapagos Islands we sailed at dusk on a clear night. Spook called chow soon after the sails were set, and we sat down to eat as Albatross turned southwest in an easy sea. The gimballed dinner table swung slowly, gently, as we ate and talked of good times and good friends found in Panama. The interest of the crew turned from the sparkling islands of the Caribbean to the dark islands of the Galapagos.

After supper I went on deck; the relaxed helmsman had one arm hooked around a spoke of the wheel, his head thrown back to see the squaresails in the last red light of the sunset. We were on a port tack; the jibs and main rode stiffly in a good eight knots of breeze. Two or three of the crew lay sprawled on the aft lockers, murmuring animatedly of everything and nothing. I made my way to the high side of the ship where I sat on deck with my back against the center skylights. The land slipped slowly under the evening horizon, became a pale gray shape and was gone. We were once again at sea, separate from the land, back in our private world.

I lit a cigar and watched the stars appear. They came magically, first one, then two or three. Suddenly there was a whole heaven of sparkling pinpoints of light as full darkness settled upon the sea. Albatross sang liquidly through the dark, warm waters, leaving a bubbling phosphorescent wake like millions of tiny diamonds stretching on the surface as far astern as I could see. I puffed gently on my cigar, watching the red glow of the ash, enjoying fully the grand beauty of the night and content at being in that place at that time.

Skipper was on deck now. I heard as if from a long way away the changing of the watch; Skipper told a couple of the crew it might be a good time to get some star sights, and in a few minutes the conversation became excited about what stars to choose and who would use which sextant.

Then the moon began its rise, and I sat facing it as this happened. At first, just dim, wide light on the horizon brightened the small, shimmering whitecaps. Majestically, the full, stark whiteness of it rose, then the light of the full moon filled the world. Rising higher, it seemed to become a little smaller but many times brighter and whiter. It was harder to see the stars now. They were there but dimmed by the brilliance of the moon.

The wide, quicksilver path from the ship to the moon looked almost solid, almost like snow. I leaned back my head and looked straight up through the four taut squaresails, listened to the creaking, softly moaning blocks and rigging. The stars hung along the foremast and danced up and down the ratlines as Albatross rocked smoothly, steadily through the gently hissing seas. One of the crew was standing on a footrope, high aloft, silhouetted against the ivory squaresails and I knew that someone else was enchanted by the night.

Skipper sat beside me. I did not want to talk. "It's great, isn't it?" I grunted in reply and took a long pull at my cigar. Skipper stretched his legs and scratched his head, looking sideways at me but saying nothing more. We remained silent for a long while, each with his own thoughts.

Skipper at last spoke. "Guess I'll turn in. Must be late."

I didn't want to leave. Occasionally someone passed, stepped over my outstretched legs, made his way forward to the galley for coffee or to the bow to chat with the watch. The night was brighter than ever, the sky absolutely clear. Albatross made her way through that joyful night, white foam and phosphorescence tumbling from her bow. I felt I was a part of the ship and the night and all the ships and nights that had ever been. I knew I would remember and be grateful for that night and afterwards compare it with other nights on other ships on other seas.

Two cigars and several hours later I arose stiffly and made myself go below to my bunk. Albatross rocked me gently, easily asleep with the sound of the surging sea a few inches from my ear, my head and my heart still filled with the glory of that white and silvery night.

After that, the voyage to the Galapagos Islands was slow, much of the time under power. The crew caught large tuna and dolphin, which Spook prepared in delicious wine and cheese sauces. During occasional rain showers some of us washed clothes in fresh water caught in buckets and the longboats. Porpoises played about the bow. We heard their high, thin squealing and watched them leap and twist by the hour.

After supper Spook would usually join me forward on deck for a cigar and conversation. We discussed short stories and plays, people we had met, a boat of our own in which we would cruise the world. One of Spook's favorite ideas, though, was to open a restaurant in Baja California. During the three years he'd spent on *Albatross* he'd sent home hundreds of sea shells and pieces of driftwood collected from beaches of Africa and the Caribbean as decorations. It would have been a fine restaurant, had he lived to open it.

We staged the traditional initiation to the kingdom of King Neptune as we crossed the equator. Only Spook, Skipper, Alice and I were already members, and we needed help initiating the rest of the crew. Spook's Davy Jones costume was a work of art: a painted sea shell in one eye, a popcorn beard, a shark-tooth necklace and on each hand a turtle flipper. The purpose of the flippers was quickly revealed. As he strode about the deck calling for all hands to lay aft and hear his message from Neptune, he flipped away at the boys' rear ends and heads. Soon he had everyone gathered about his throne next to the wheelhouse and read a message from Neptune.

"Hear ye! The day of reckoning is at hand! On the morrow His Ultimate Majesty King Neptune, Lord of the Seas, Ruler of the Green Depths and Grand Potentate of the Piscatorial Palaces will board *Albatross*! Stand all ye in dread of his coming! The ignominious crew of said *Albatross* for these several months past has raped and pillaged its way through the Kingdom of the Deep, abducting and eating the flesh of Neptune's people and must now stand to account for its heinous crimes."

The message continued, saying that Davy Jones was present to punish three of the worst offenders — J.C., Bill, and John. Punishments imposed always fit the crimes; personality traits and likes and dislikes are considered. Bill had to kiss the deck because he was first mate, then hang by his heels over the side and receive a drenching from a bucketful of turtle blood that Spook had "cured" for weeks behind the galley stove. John had his head shaved because he had refused haircuts from port to port and had grown a thick, shaggy mop of hair. J.C. was forced to kick to pieces a copy of Time Magazine (his favorite) and, as ship's mathematician, had to measure the length of *Albatross* from stem to stern and all the way up the foremast.

Various other indignities were imposed, but they got off lightly compared to the rest of the crew when King Neptune boarded the next day. I was King Neptune in royal robes made from two large beach towels plus a straw hat and dark glasses. With my shark-vertebrae cane and a foot-long cigar I even frightened myself when I looked into a mirror below.

Alice worked out some imaginative crimes and punishments for me to read from a scroll: two boys who disliked each other were tied together for a day; the boy with the untidiest bunk had to put all of his clothes into a pillow case and climb the mainmast ratlines, tying one article of clothing to each step as he climbed; large eaters were dressed as pigs and made to go without food for 24 hours; a dedicated souvenir collector was instructed to put the contents of the storage area in the forepeak into his bunk, neatly. The shyest, most diffident boy became Demosthenes the orator, compelled to climb to the very top of the foremast and orate for an hour about the beauties and grandeur of Neptune's Kingdom. Inveterate fishermen fished from buckets, late risers were awakened every hour from sound sleep, and a couple of boys who invariably failed to fill in the ship's log as they came off watch were instructed to sign the log every hour for a day and a night. The weary crew happily received their Shellback certificates to prove that they had crossed the equator.

Our first landfall after nine days at sea was Rock Redondo. The high, straight, pointed rock looked like a huge sail sticking up from the bottom of the ocean, the last remnant above water of a volcanic cone. Melville describes it in The Encantadas: "Here and there were long birdlime streaks of a ghostly white staining the tower from sea to air, readily accounting for its sail-like look afar." Rock Redondo can be seen from 30 miles away and is easily mistaken for a ship.

After formally entering the Galapagos Islands at the tiny fishing village of Wreck Bay, we cruised to Barrington Island, which is inhabited only by goats, birds and sea lions.

We lay to in a small, quiet cove, one anchor out astern and another from the bow to hold us in water deep enough to keep us off the bottom. The reef was a playground for sea lions; dozens dragged around over the rocks and swam along the edges. The females were flirtatious and swam with us, sometimes diving between our legs and suddenly coming out of the water just a foot in front of us to blow water in our faces. They seemed delighted to have strangers to play with. Few males were around. They were larger, had brown furry coats instead of the sleek black of the females and were not as friendly.

Late in the afternoon *Albatross* was covered with large black flies, millions of them. Skipper told us they had hatched in the bodies of dead sea lions and birds on the island. We had to wear clothing on deck from late afternoon until a few minutes after sunset, when they disappeared. Not a single fly remained aboard at night. Next day they appeared again in great swarms, and in order to hold classes we had to cover the companionways and skylights with cheesecloth. Even so, thousands collected in the main cabin where we ate. I soon acquired a second nickname — General Bugbomb — for insisting we spray insecticide in the main cabin before meals.

On the first night at Barrington I sat on deck after supper. The sky was clear; the starlight was bright enough to light the white beach at one end of the cove, and I could see the little female sea lions flopping about the shore and in the surf. From over the lava ridge toward the sea I heard rocks knocking about and some grunts and squeals. I had no idea what was making the commotion.

Alice said it sounded like two male sea lions fighting, a younger one challenging an older one for his crown. The battle continued for hours. In the morning I rowed to the little sand beach. Sitting in the warm sun with a dozen or more lovely, sleek females cavorting before him was the winner and new champion of Barrington, erect, proud, battle-scarred and very much in command.

There is no effective way to prepare for meeting the

Galapagos Islands. I read Darwin, Beebe, Melville and many articles about the islands before I saw them, but the fantastic colors and shapes and surfaces were beyond my powers to imagine them. Melville wrote, "Take five-and-twenty heaps of cinders dumped here and there in an outside city lot; imagine some of them magnified into mountains, and the vacant lot the sea; and you will have a fit idea of the general aspect of the Encantadas, or Enchanted Isles."

A group of recently active volcanoes owned by Ecuador, the Galapagos Islands lie directly on the equator. They have no change of season, almost no rain, and the dry heat and ashy black-lava surface of most of them makes animal life there very difficult. Each kind of bird, turtle, goat, penguin, sea lion, and iguana had to develop a special way to survive. The adaptive process was noted by Darwin and confirmed his famous evolutionary theories.

Humans, too, must adapt to the Enchanted Isles. Not many live there, but all who do have learned to take the islands as they found them. A good example is the Wittmer family who dwelled on Floreana for some 35 years. Down on the coast of the island the Wittmers constructed two or three houses of scrap lumber and rocks and make a living by fishing from a small boat they built themselves. Mrs. Wittmer writes stories and books about Floreana and has sold them to magazines and publishing houses all over the world. High in the mountains behind their houses they have a small farm where they raise fruits and vegetables. There's not much rain, but what there is falls on top of the mountains, so it's necessary to hike several miles into the hills to farm successfully. Thus, with produce from the farm and fish from the sea, they manage to live well enough. There are few visitors - an occasional boat stops out of curiosity - but they live a full life using all of their talents and energies every day.

Forest Nelson had a rather comfortable life near Academy Bay, at least comfortable by Galapagos standards. He and Mrs. Nelson installed a kind of shower using water brought down from the mountains in a sluice, plus a kerosene-powered refrigerator (true luxury). They kept big bottles of fine Ecuadorian beer in the refrigerator, and I enjoyed several afternoons drinking the beer and discussing the islands. Forest was building a couple of stone cottages on the beach near his house for any visitors who might want to stay ashore for an extended period.

Forest is an American who moved to the Galapagos Islands and married a pretty Swedish girl he met there. He told me he was cruising the islands on his boat, Nellie Brush, met his future bride, took her with him to California, married her, and returned to the islands to live. Local legend has it that the young man who had expected all his life to marry the girl just gave up interest in eating and died in a few months of malnutrition.

It all has the ring of truth. Marriageable girls are hard to find in the Galapagos Islands, and supposedly the young boy and girl had been raised from childhood on adjoining mountain farms in the certain knowledge that they would some day marry. But Forest came along and ended the idyll.

The Galapagos Islands are a great, wide, infinitely varied laboratory for studying wildlife. *Albatross'* crew studied marine and land iguanas, small penguins that had migrated up the Humboldt current from the South Pole, sea lions, and every imaginable form of fish. There were nine-foot sharks, porpoises, giant manta rays, crayfish, crabs, small octopuses, a half-dozen kinds of small, edible fish, and sea turtles and huge land tortoises. We even gathered sea plankton in tiny nets for microscopic study. The birds were beautiful and quite tame. They flew all around the ship, often alighting in the rigging. Finches, boobies, albatrosses, frigates, gulls, pelicans - all could be studied closely. The crew made pets of several penguins and iguanas that had the run of the ship while we cruised.

We looked forward to going ashore and seeing the big barrel at Post Office Bay, used by sailors as a mailbox for generations. Skipper told us that mail left in the barrel still would be picked up by other passing ships and delivered eventually to any place in the world, just as had been done when 19th-century whalers and merchantmen had used the barrel. Some of the crew wanted to repair and paint the barrel, so brushes, paint, hammers and nails were put into a longboat. A heavy swell was roaring up the beach, and we trailed the dinghy behind the longboat to use in ferry service. Several boys dove in and swam ashore.

I jumped onto the soft, wet sand from the dinghy and moved quickly up the beach ahead of the next charge of foaming surf just behind me. Iguanas scurried over the loose rocks to hide or perhaps escape the dry, burning heat. The morning was clear with no wind, and the sun bore down heavily. There was no shade, no trees to get under, and the ashy, rocky ground and brittle, brown weeds and brush were like a desert.

I spotted the barrel. It was covered with the names of boats that had stopped at Post Office Bay. The rocks beneath it were littered with the dry, white skeletons of iguanas, goats, turtles and birds, looking as if they had been put there as offerings to ensure the safe delivery of letters left in the barrel.

The boys began their work, scraping and painting the barrel. Someone painted a sign - *Albatross* 1961 - to be attached to the barrel just before we left.

I walked slowly over the hot, dry sand and rocks through the thorny brush toward what seemed to be a large concrete block. It was actually a huge, rectangular concrete form 15 feet long and two feet across, and there were several scattered around the area. Most had been haphazardly dropped in various positions, but some were in rows as though they had served as the foundation for a building. There were other signs of human presence, left behind years ago as attempts to colonize Post Office Bay had failed. I saw pots, jars and a few battered kitchen utensils lying on the rocks, with weeds growing through and over them. In the center of a partially cleared area were two large metal structures. One was a nearly triangular iron pot lying on its side, at least five feet high and rusted dark brown by the years of island exposure. The other was a large, rectangular box or bin about 10 feet long and six wide; both had been simply abandoned to the iguanas, wild goats and turtles. I hadn't expected to find all this human detritus.

What surprised me most was the sight of several acres laid out in city squares. Big blocks of lava had been brought down from the hills surrounding the area and had been carefully placed in long lines as curbstones to mark roads. A complete park-like square occupied the center, with roads running eight directions from the corners into the wild, desolate land beyond. I walked along one of them, with the sharp lava crunching under foot until the road divided about 300 yards down one branch. I thought of the men who must have sweated untold hours beneath a glaring sun to build a road to nowhere.

Why would anyone build roads in such a forsaken place? There were no cars, not even a horse or a donkey, nothing to use the roads except perhaps a land tortoise or iguana, who could hardly appreciate the cost in human labor that must have gone into the roads. There isn't even any water on the island except very high in the mountains, miles away and nearly unobtainable. The entire location was dreary, dry, gloomy, desolate place, totally unfit for man.

The sun stood higher, became hotter. The lava dust and ash arose in small clouds as I walked back to the central part of what might have begun as a town. I felt depressed and saddened, as if I'd found the remains of a lost civilization that once had been great and glorious but now had disappeared from the earth.

The Spanish have always called these bleak islands Encantadas, the Enchanted Isles. There are strong and unpredictable currents nearby, and early mariners found it difficult to make for a particular part of the islands and count on reaching it accurately. Sometimes an island gives false impressions concerning its shape or size and its distance from the observer because of thermal currents in the hot, dry air. As Melville points out, early charts of the area showed two sets of islands instead of one because, depending upon the currents, tides and time of the year, the Galapagos seemed to be in varying longitudes. Thus the islands appeared to move around and were thought to be enchanted.

The United States had an airbase near Academy Bay during World War II, but it was released to Ecuador after the war. They dismantled it, many of the natives and settlers taking various furnishings to use in their own homes; a few tore down whole barracks to get the lumber. In recent years the government restored parts of the airbase, and occasionally a government plane lands there. Most transportation, though, is by the monthly mail boat from the mainland some 800 miles away.

Several days later, still thinking about the dreariness of Post Office Bay, I spoke to Gus Angermeyer about it. Gus and his family had lived in the Galapagos Islands more than 30 years and no one knows the history of the islands any better than he. Gus was short, heavy and gifted with a barrel chest. He had black hair, dark eyes set deeply in his large head and a face brown and creased from long days in the hot sun.

Gus had a way of looking at you when he talked that disturbed people not accustomed to simple, frank answers to their questions. He and his two brothers had come to the Galapagos Islands from Germany in the 1930s.

"Many people try to colonize these islands," Gus said. "Most give up after a few months. They do not understand about living here. They come for the wrong reasons, perhaps to escape something they do not like in their own country. But they must not do that. They must come to live here with this world as it is. They are bored or unhappy. They want to get away from all that upsets them. But it will be no better here unless they are ready to work very hard just to live. They must come here because they want to use all of themselves before they die."

Gus learned how to live in the Galapagos, meeting life on its own terms. He was a fisherman and hunter, taking just what he and his family needed. Like Thoreau, he avoided carrying the luxuries of civilization on his back, and I came to admire him. He was well-read and enjoyed good music. The whole family speaks several languages, and every day is complete in itself as an adventure in living. Gus has built his own house, his boat, and educated his children without the special tools and methods of more comfortable parts of the world.

"Sometimes they write to me from Europe to ask about living out here," he said with a grin. "Some of you writers make it sound like more fun than work. They ask about our schools, stores, doctors. One woman asked if we had a newspaper. I tell all the people who ask for these things that they must not come here; they would starve. Sometimes they do not believe me and come anyway. When the wife becomes pregnant, they leave."

Gus looked out across Academy Bay and squinted his eyes at a gull skimming over the water, hunting for food. "Do you see that bird? He must work all day to get enough to eat. So must I. And so must the people who come here. It is very hard. The ruins you saw at Post Office Bay — some Scandinavians came out here many years before my brother and I, and they wanted to build a fine city and catch whales. They brought their civilization with them. But there was no water or food here except what they caught from the sea, and the whales were few. So they left. They did not want to live in such a hard place. But I do not think they would be satisfied anywhere. They were not ready to live in the Galapagos Islands; they wanted to live in a dream they had in their heads. One lives here as just one more Galapagos animal or one does not live here. One does not change the islands."

Gus sat upon an outcropping of lava, wiping the sweat from his forehead with the back of his hand. "Did you see the abandoned cannery over at Wreck Bay?" I had. "Some Ecuadorians brought it out by ship some years back. It has a lot of freezing and canning equipment and barracks and houses for workers. They thought they could live an easy life, freeze fish for the mainland. But they missed the life on the mainland

and fought each other and took each other's wives, and it was all finished in a few months. They came to make a fortune and then go back home. These islands will not allow that. Those people might have been all right here if they had thought of the islands as their home. But, like the Americans, they came for the wrong reasons."

The Americans were from the West Coast, Oregon, I think, and had been brought out by a flim-flam artist who told them they were going to a Pacific paradise where they would have a simple, romantic life. Several hundred sold their homes, raised all the cash they could and gave most of it to the dishonest broker. They arrived with electric stoves, irons, refrigerators, stoves, washing machines and other electrical appliances with which to set up housekeeping. Of course there was no electricity. All the appliances ended in a big junk pile, eventually left to rust. In a few weeks most had had enough of lava, sun and iguanas and were ready to return to the United States. Few had any money, so it took the combined efforts of the Ecuadorian government and United States diplomatic service to get them back. Only one family remained.

As I came topside one morning, I saw Alice dressed to go ashore in a bright red skirt and blue blouse. Her MD satchel sat on one of the stern lockers with a large cardboard box of medical supplies. She checked the box of supplies and called to Gus, who was waiting for her in his little motorboat. "I'm almost ready, Gus. Be with you in a minute."

She looked around and said, "Big Daddy, will you hand this box over to Gus? I hope I don't need all this stuff, but I might as well have it, just in case."

"Where are you off to?"

"House calls. It's been three years since anyone in Academy Bay has seen a doctor, and Gus has a list of people waiting to see me. I treated a dozen families last time we were out here on *Yankee*. Everything from impetigo to heart conditions."

I handed the box down to Gus; in honor of the occasion he wore a blue denim shirt and a clean pair of khaki shorts. Alice climbed over the rail and lowered herself into the boat and off they went to visit the sick of Academy Bay. Late in the afternoon I heard the little boat sputter alongside. Alice had spent the whole day treating the local folk and instructing them in proper sanitation and eating habits.

The arrival of *Albatross* was important to the people of the Galapagos. Not only did we bring Alice and her medicines but a floating supermarket as well. On two mornings the ladies of the village came aboard to shop for canned goods unobtainable locally. Alice had seen to it that extra supplies were brought aboard just for this purpose when we loaded at Panama. The villagers appreciated the rare chance to buy canned fruits and vegetables, which they carted away in bags and cartons.

Alice and Skipper also gave away dozens of magazines and newspapers; reading material was scarce, and it didn't matter that most were months old. We heard from Forest Nelson that the best-read treatise in the Galapagos Islands was the Sears & Roebuck catalog. It was filled with items that would make life a little easier for them if they could be obtained, and families turned the pages until it disintegrated in their hands. It reminded me of much that I had read about the American West and farm families ordering from Sears. In the Enchanted Isles, though, even if a family saved enough to buy something, it was months before it could be delivered. But these people had learned patience. A year was not too long to wait for a new saw or an outboard motor or bright cloth for a shirt.

Surprises occurred every day. The penguins, booby birds, sea lions, tortoises, iguanas, sharks and manta rays all were creatures in books until I faced and touched them.

The people -- the Angermeyers, Wittmers, Nelsons, and the dozens of Ecuadorians -- were most surprising of all. They had come to terms with their strange world, something very difficult for most of us to do. We try to dominate the world instead of living in it, and in the end the world dominates us.

The Galapagos Islands are young, geologically

speaking. Active volcanoes have been seen in the area as recently as the 1930s, and only the older islands have vegetation on them. Some are completely covered with lava rock without so much as a weed growing on them. As the centuries pass and the seas wash over low spots leaving sea weed and minerals and animal matter, as a little rain falls, life on land begins.

Frequently one sees such a low area, perhaps in the center of an island, where birds drop their guano, where rain and seeds fall. In time, weeds grow, more birds nest, more rain falls, and after many years a thick grove of cactus and brush is created.

Such a place is James Island, where Spook and I climbed a volcano and looked down to see a tiny patch of green in the lowest part of the island near the beach. For miles in every other direction there was nothing but the charred lava hills. Many years from now, if the world lasts long enough, the Galapagos Islands may look like the Hawaiian Islands-a tropical paradise.

The sun was already hot at 9 a.m. on the morning Spook and I decided to climb the extinct volcano at James Island. We dressed in shorts and sneakers, took along caps to keep our heads shaded, and shoved off in the dinghy. After beaching it in the hot sand and slinging our canvas camera bags over our shoulders, we set out across the sharp, brittle lava surface, pushing through wiry bramble and cactus toward the slopes of the volcano. A dry breeze blew across the crusty ground, and we stopped frequently to empty the rocky ash from our sneakers.

Careful climbing was necessary. There was razor-sharp rock under our feet; and a fall would hurt us badly. The volcano was covered with loose, sliding shale and hunks of oddly shaped blue, black, and red slag-like lava. Some had cooled from its molten state into weird shapes and curves. In places it looked like thickly swirled black icing.

We moved very slowly past wide holes that opened straight down into the mountain. Spook paused at one that measured at least 12 feet across and dropped a chunk of slag into it. We heard it rumble and clank as it fell but did not detect it hitting bottom. A smaller hole had a "lid" just above it like a manhole with a hinged cover standing open. Hot gas and lava had blown through the side of the volcano just as the lava had begun to cool, leaving the lid frozen open, eternal testimony to the violent, hell-hot explosions that must have occurred here years ago as the islands were rising from the ocean's floor.

As we climbed we sometimes bent double to balance ourselves. Our feet slid in all directions on the loose, broken lava; it was like walking on millions of pieces of broken crockery. It clicked and clanked and tumbled down the mountain as we gradually moved higher and higher.

There was no relief from the dry heat of the brilliant sun; the black rocks absorbed the heat, making us feel that we were walking over hot coals. We could see the summit now and headed toward it along a lava ridge that was almost smooth, with little mounds and swirls in it. It seemed solid, but Spook poked his staff through it easily. It was just a thin crust, bubble-like, and we had to be careful not to step too heavily and break through. I thought of the bottomless pit into which Spook had thrown the piece of slag.

On top, I felt as if I were standing above the earth. There was no plant life, of course, nothing but dry, bare, black lava extending down the volcano on all sides as far as I could see. *Albatross*, lying to anchor below, looked like a tiny toy, and we could just make out the dinghy on the postage-stamp beach. It was barely a speck on the dark sand, and if we had not known where to look, we couldn't have seen it.

I set up my camera on a tripod and took several pictures using the delayed-action timer so Spook and I could both get into the pictures. The sun shining upon the black lava made excellent contrast, and some of the pictures are startlingly clear and sharp. About 2,000 feet beneath us, down the nearly sheer drop to the sea, the surf burst white up the black lava, foaming and roaring faintly. It moved grandly, gracefully, almost in slow motion.

Sitting on the lava bed, I got out my rigging knife and cut my one cigar in half. We smoked and talked. In a little valley of rock and black sand, toward the center of the volcano, there were several ship's names spelled out in large rocks brought one at a time to create the letters. I could make out Irving Johnson's *Yankee* and Forest Nelson's *Nellie Brush.* There were others, but I do not remember them. Spook suggested we scatter the rocks and restore the area to a condition something like it was before human egos had reshaped it, but it would have been very hot work and we decided against it. Surrounding the little valley were three large cones about 100 feet high, open at the top where lava and hot gases had belched from deep inside the volcano.

We began our descent. It was harder getting down than getting up; we nearly lost our balance several times, and the loose shale slid from beneath our feet at the smallest misstep. Spook thought he saw a safer way down, so he headed away from me. I continued going down the same way I had gone up. In a few minutes we were several hundred yards apart; Spook was walking along a ridge, staff in hand, cap down over his eyes, his thin, slightly bent figure looking much like that of an Arab walking slowly across the desert.

I slipped and scrambled along, gradually working my way down the mountain. My left foot was extended before me, my body turned to the right, and I leaned backwards toward the mountain at a very steep place. Suddenly my left foot broke through the lava crust, caught, and the weight of my body pressed down on it at an angle. I felt my ankle crack. The foot turned under completely, and I tumbled face-first down the slope, my hands and knees taking most of the punishment. My shoulder hit heavily against a large hunk of lava and sent it crashing and tumbling down the mountainside, but I was able to get a hold on the lava crust with my hands.

I cut the long strap from my camera bag and straightened the ankle, wrapping the strap firmly under the arch of my sneaker and around the ankle to immobilize it as best I could. Then I stood, putting most of my weight on my right leg. The ankle was becoming painful but still I could use it. I began a long, slow descent down the volcano, pausing frequently to rest, sometimes hopping a few yards on one foot, sometimes sliding along on my rear end at more dangerous spots. Another fall might finish me, and I moved very cautiously.

Reaching the beach at last, I removed the strap and sneaker from the injured foot and watched the swelling increase. It was like watching a balloon expand. In a few minutes my ankle and lower leg was as large as my thigh. I removed the other sneaker and dragged myself into the water to soak and waited for Spook. He came along in a few minutes, smiling at the way I sat in the water.

When I explained matters to him, he said, "Big Daddy, people as big as you ought to have bigger ankles."

He dragged the dinghy to the water, helped me into it and rowed back to *Albatross*. Alice cast the ankle and leg a day later after some of the swelling had reduced. I sat atop the charthouse dangling the leg so it would be at a good height for Alice. She did a fine job, even putting in a rubber doorstop under my heel as a sort of walker so I could get around. Later I rigged a sling so I could stand my watch by sitting on the wheelhouse, with the leg stuck out to port and supported by a rope attached to the main boom gallows.

Albatross anchored in dozens of coves and along lava beaches as we sailed from island to island. Gus came aboard for a few days to lead the crew on a search for land tortoises. His son Johnny, 16, stayed a week and attended most of our classes and taught our crew about his islands. Each morning was usually given over to schoolwork seven days a week, so we could get in enough class periods for certification. Afternoons were often free unless Skipper had some special project that needed attention. For her part, Alice gave the stern rail and seat lockers a going-over with sandpaper and three coats of varnish.

One day-long expedition was to see the giant Galapagos tortoises. Venerable animals, many are old enough to have a 100-year-old growth of green algae and mold on their shells. Gus told us they often lived to be 300 and sometimes weighed as much as 600 pounds. Melville says they were used as fresh meat by 19th-century whalers and could live a year in the hold of a ship without food, so slow is their metabolism. The heavy, oval-shaped creatures lumber slowly and awkwardly over the lava crusts and through thick bushes, always in a straight line. "Their crowning curse is their drudging impulse to straightforwardness in a belittered world," says Melville.

Some of the crew climbed aboard the backs of the tortoises and tried to ride them but the great beasts could rarely be prodded into a pace any faster than their usual one.

Anchored in Darwin Bay, we went ashore to see the bird rookery. We found thousands of frigate and booby nests just a few yards up from the beach. It was a furiously active scene with the huge birds flying, landing, walking, strutting, stretching their wings, uttering cacophonous cries, and some were sitting calmly in their nests ignoring all the confusion and motion around them.

Some of the frigates strutted stiffly in short circles, wings outstretched, the large, bright red, balloon-like membrane under their necks inflated and puffed out as a sign they were ready to mate, should a female be willing. Others had found a mate, ensconced her in the grass and were off to find nest-building materials. As often as not, they walked over the brambles to the nearest booby nest and stole twigs from it.

Many nests contained eggs. One could walk right up to the sitting birds, push the female off the nest, take a picture of the eggs, and the bird would climb back on the nest as if nothing had happened. None of the birds were afraid of us. They simply ignored our intrusion.

For supper that night we ate large, succulent crayfish which the crew had caught by diving for them in the Bay. They are much like the so-called Florida lobster, only larger. Spook served them boiled with lemon sauce, and Newburg-style. Fish are easy to catch in the Enchanted Isles; all one needs is a line and a hook with a bit of colored rag on it to attract the fish's attention. We often took dozens of one- to two-pound trout-like fish in just a few minutes. Gus caught thousands, drying and salting them for shipment to Ecuador and as food for his family the year around.

A crew member spotted a manta ray from the foretop as we neared Tagus Cove one day. As soon as the anchor was down, we lowered a longboat and some of the crew gave chase. Within an hour they threw gang hooks ahead of him and finally snared him near one of his two eyes. The eyes protruded from each side of his wide mouth on long stalks. It took another hour to work him close enough to *Albatross* to tie him to the bowsprit.

The manta was powerful; his long, wide, gray and white wings undulated ceaselessly as he swam in a slow circle beneath the bowsprit. The boys donned sweat suits and tried to ride him. He dove to get rid of them but they held on tightly to his tail or just above his open mouth. Some of us watched him swim that night. It was a dark night with no moon, and the water was black. The ray swam untiringly in his small circle under the bow, and thousands of small fish had come to watch the big ray as he swam literally at the end of his tether.

I was sorry about the manta ray. I know Alice wanted it for her biology class the next day and I understood that the boys would learn a lot from studying it. But I was still sorry about it: millions of years of evolution culminating in this impressive, frighteningly beautiful creature would be obliterated. I watched for a very long time before I went below to bed. Next morning the ray was still swimming. Skipper brought him alongside and the boys shot him with rifles and lifted him on deck with the boat boom. He measured over 14 feet from wing tip to wing tip and must have weighed about 2000 pounds. His gray skin was furry and tough, almost like the hide of an old elephant or range steer. Alice said he was relatively young and small, that such rays when full grown could have a wing span of 30 feet and might weigh as much as 5000 pounds. When biology class began, I went below.

One evening we said our good-byes to our friends in Academy Bay and began the long haul back to Panama. Gus rode a short way, and we trailed his little boat behind us. Some knew we would never see him again, and Gus realized it would be years before Skipper and Alice might return. We watched for a long while as he headed back to Academy Bay. I turned in early because my watch began at midnight.

We touched bottom about 11 p.m; the steel hull shuddered and rumbled. From a deep sleep I was instantly, rigidly awake, frozen in my bunk. I hardly breathed, wondering if we would hit again.

Another bump, and *Albatross* seemed to rise an inch or two as she plowed heavily over the bottom. Scrambling feet thumped on deck as Skipper shouted, "Engine room — slow ahead! Get a leadline forward!" The big diesel slowed to a dull, distant throbbing as the leadsman's calls came from just above me.

"Four fathoms!" There was a pause, then the splash of the lead as it hit the water again.

"Three-and-a-half!"

"Three fathoms!"

We had only seven feet of water under our keel now.

It held at three. Then came the call at four, then five, and the leadline was secured. I wiped the perspiration from my face and dried my palms on a towel. J.C. tapped lightly on the panel between our bunks and leaned his head toward me.

"What the hell was that?"

"You got me. Guess we hit some mud. Lucky it wasn't rock." We both got up. Neither of us said it but I knew we felt better on deck. Land lay very close off to port, a high, hulking black mass. At breakfast we learned from some of the watch that *Albatross* had changed course a little too soon and thumped over some mud. In the daylight, full of good food and on the open sea, we laughed about it. Tod suggested we name a new drink in honor of the occasion: *Albatross* on the Rocks. Skipper tried to smile.

This wasn't the only time we escaped possible serious

injury or damage. A longboat fell as it was lowered over the side. Often one of the crew rode in the boats to handle the tackle, but fortunately no one was in this one. Once we nearly lost our anchor and *Albatross* when a link snapped on the chain. Again we were lucky. Skipper swam down to check the chain because we had swung completely around during the night, anchored in heavy swells off a long lava reef. He found the broken link, miraculously still holding. He went back down with a line and tied it below the break. With the line wrapped around the deck winch he took off the strain as we hoisted the anchor.

Remembering my Joseph Conrad, I took all these and other similar episodes as additional evidence for his contention that we are all "eternally menaced, most of all by ourselves." A moment's carelessness or neglect, or a smug sense of well-being can often lead to disaster.

The voyage back to Panama took 10 days, mostly under power. I had plenty of time to think about the fascinating places and people we had met in the Galapagos Islands. The contrast between life in the West Indies and the Enchanted Isles was graphic. The Caribbean was green and friendly; the Galapagos Islands were hard and cold. The people in the former were warm, soft, and lived easily; in the latter they were guarded, tough, isolated, and sweated hard for their living. The Windward and Leeward Islands were already a part of our civilization, but the Galapagos Islands were still coming into being, physically and socially. I had enjoyed the Caribbean fully and appreciated its lush, tropical life and laughing people, but I had also learned to admire the pioneer courage and elemental existence of those strong, lonely inhabitants of the black volcanic mountains of the Encantadas.

Once back in Panama for mail and supplies, Alice let me remove the cast from my leg, and after a few hours I could get around rather well with a cane. I had a good supply of them now and could choose any color or type I liked. After several days of rest and visits to Panama City we made our way back through the Canal and sailed for the islands of the

San Blas Indians off the east coast of Panama.

The islands are very small grass-covered plots of land, most no larger than a few acres. The people are still very primitive and dislike the invasion of civilization to the extent that no whites are allowed to remain there overnight. We were told that white men had been killed for trying to stay ashore as recently as 10 or 12 years before. Still, the San Blas were a pleasure to visit. The residents treated us kindly, showed us their grass houses with hammocks hanging inside, posed for pictures (a quarter per picture) and demonstrated their primitive cooking utensils. Some of the young boys even played basketball with our crew.

San Blas women outnumbered the men about 10 to one, so it was a matriarchal society in which the men did no work. They sat and smoked, occasionally fished a little, but mostly slept and ate. Many of the women were shy and tried to cover their faces when outsiders looked at them or tried to take a photo, especially if one failed to offer a quarter to add to their silver-coin necklaces.

As many as 200 Indians might live on a few acres of land, surrounded by water, in the grass and board huts with dirt floors. The women make beautiful mats and cloths called *molas* with intricate figures in several colors stitched on them by hand. Some of the boys and men carved oddly shaped decorative spears. I bought many of the multicolored cloths and a dozen or more of the spears to use as gifts.

In front of one large hut sat an old man reputed to be a magician or the witch doctor. I offered a cigar. He smiled broadly and offered a well-worn spear about five feet long in return. I accepted. One young man who could speak a little English told me the spear was very special and had been used in burial ceremonies to transport souls to heaven, an expression of respect from one doctor to another. (The old fellow was convinced that I, too, was a spirit doctor and asked for a few hairs from my beard, which he said would be good magic.)

I had a feeling it was all a joke and that I was the butt of it, but the old man was so earnest about it that I treated it as seriously as he. I figured the burial wand might come in handy when I returned to the United States. I knew a number of people who had been dead for years but were not aware of it and could use an assist into the spirit world.

We held our usual morning classes while anchored off the San Blas Islands. It was April now, and the boys' attention was harder than ever to hold with dugouts full of brightly dressed Indians clustered all around *Albatross* during daylight hours.

Just before leaving we watched a dugout burial flotilla headed for the mainland several miles away. My friend the witch doctor sat regally in the bow of one of the larger canoes. The San Blas have no room to bury the dead and must take them ashore.

We had a brisk breeze on a starboard tack that put my bunk on the high side, and I used the bunkboard all the way to Yucatan to keep from falling out. We anchored off the small fishing village of Progresso. Half the crew went off on an excursion by taxi to Merida and the Mayan ruins of Chichen Itza and Uxmal, while the other half stayed aboard to take care of the ship. Spook had the whole time off, and he deserved it, having worked hard in the galley seven days a week for a long time.

J.C. and I went ashore with the second half of the crew and joined Spook at the Hotel Merida. All of us fell in love with Merida and had a full, exciting three-day visit in the beautiful, clean city and at the ruins. I was still limping along with the help of a cane and could not climb the pyramids at Chichen as the others did, but I enjoyed wandering around and sitting on old stone blocks and stairways that were all over the area.

In Merida we shopped at the big marketplace for sandals, Mexican silver, shirts, and grass hammocks. We hired a mariachi band to play for us at meals and even took them with us in a second horse-drawn cab when we went out to have dinner. It was a marvelous time that ended much too soon for all of us.

White Squall -- *Richard Langford*

On our last day in Merida Spook and I searched two old shops for Mayan carvings and statuary. I found a real treasure covered with cobwebs on top of a shelf: a grotesque Mayan woman giving birth in the traditional squatting position. The old, green, stone statue was intricately carved; even the painful expressions on the faces of the mother and her half-born child were done in detail.

Late one afternoon the Trinity took a taxi back to *Albatross*, loaded down with shopping bags, and we almost missed the ship's sailing (or so we thought at the time). The taxi we chose had a leaky radiator and steamed over about halfway. From then on we stopped every few minutes to find water from wells in the middle of sisal fields, from cane cutters, and from huts along the road. *Albatross* was still there when we reached Progresso, but the sun was setting and Skipper had said he would sail at dark. In desperation, the three of us hired a local fishing captain to take us out to the ship in his 60-foot trawler. It was an impressive return, a fitting end to our Mexican visit. The big trawler rolled from side to side as I braced myself with my cane, balancing my packages and camera bag. We heaved most of the gear on deck and jumped one at a time from the trawler to our ship as the two big craft came level in the pitching seas. Our special return trip was unnecessary; we did not sail until midnight. Alice and Skipper had gone ashore to have dinner with the port captain.

It was a good night for sailing. With a steady breeze off the land *Albatross* surged forward, heading for the Bahamas and home. It was to be the last good sail.

White Squall -- *Richard Langford*

chapter six
WHITE SQUALL

I had been on watch from midnight to 4 a.m. on the morning the school ship *Albatross* went down. We'd seen a lot of lightning and a long, high, black squall line to the north. When the watch was changed, I noted in the log, "Lots of celestial fireworks up north; squall coming." We didn't think it was dangerous and hoped it would bring us some wind.

Albatross was several days out of Yucatan on its way to the Bahamas, and there had been no wind since the night we left.

Homeward bound after a 10,000-mile cruise, our 14 high school and freshman college students had worked and

97

studied aboard the big square-rigger for eight months. On watches the boys talked of home, parents and friends who would meet them in the United States. Even without wind *Albatross* moved steadily along the last leg of the long voyage as her engine pushed her at five knots.

After watch I turned in for a short sleep but at 7:30 was awakened by the call for breakfast. When I sat up I noticed we were moving faster and heeling to starboard. We were under sail again, and I could hear the sea rushing past the steel hull just a few inches from my head. It was hard to climb out of my bunk, which was on the starboard or downside of the ship. At breakfast, the main cabin table tilted sharply in its gimbals as *Albatross* rolled through roughening waters. The lightning was closer, and we could hear loud booms of thunder very near. As we ate our pancakes, a few drops of rain fell through the midship skylights partially open on the lee side for ventilation.

I sat beside Christopher Sheldon, our skipper and head of Ocean Academy Ltd. His wife Alice, biology teacher and ship's surgeon, sat on the other side. A drop of rain hit Skipper on the nose. He looked up through a skylight and said, "We might get some fun out of that in a little while. Good to hear the wind again." We got something out of it, all right.

After breakfast I returned to my bunk to read and write. The ship heeled farther to starboard, and I could hear seawater sloshing across the deck above. I never really got used to that sound. Whenever I climbed into my bunk with water on deck, I felt as though I were climbing into my coffin. I had suggested the analogy several times to Spook. The idea bothered him, too.

Though he had cooked aboard *Albatross* for over three years, Spook had told me more than once he couldn't shake off the idea that he'd someday be caught beneath the water. I'm sorry now that I ever smiled at his fear. Spook asked me to help find a one-man life raft and survival kit to keep in his cabin. He was a creative cook who prepared all manner of delicious fare aboard ship. Often he was up before dawn to make fresh doughnuts or coffee cake, and would laugh gleefully when he succeeded in making more than the ship's company could eat.

Spook enjoyed his work. In fact, he enjoyed every part of it, and all of us appreciated his enthusiasm and unfailing kindnesses. His lean, brown face and black hair was a welcome sight every day as he made his way to the galley.

The wind pressed our brigantine farther to starboard, and green water poured into my bunk. I shouted to J. C. in the bunk just aft of me, "I'm soaked — all my books!"

Both of us realized the danger at the same moment and scrambled down from our bunks in our underwear. We stared at each other in disbelief and tried to stay on our feet in the nearly capsized vessel.

I shouted to J.C., as if he could do something, "Put her off! Why don't they put her off? They'll sink us!"

Skipper had already given that order, but it was too late.

Before *Albatross* could answer her helm and turn down wind, she was on her side. She lay flat in the churning seas, shoved down by a savage wind in her topsail like a huge tree blown down in a hurricane. Her squaresails and great mainsail filled with tons of sea water, and she would not rise again.

The five watertight steel compartments were useless. Upright, she could have floated even with her hull ripped open. But lying on her side, her open companionways and skylights were level with the sea, and green water roared in.

She filled in seconds. Two students, Tom and Bob, were in the forward compartment with J.C. and me. Tad, another student, leaped in from the main cabin the instant *Albatross* was on her side, and the five of us started forward through a narrow passage toward the forepeak, a tiny storage area in the very bow of the ship. A wheel from Bob's dismantled bike fell against my back. A scuba tank rolled down from a bunk and plunged into the water just ahead of me. I lurched to one side, and my hand broke through the plastic cover of one of the overhead passageway lights that were down near my knees by now.

I was last in line. We climbed over typewriters, canned goods and bedding that washed around in the seawater. Boys started to push forward faster, and I heard J.C. say, "All right, don't panic. Don't panic."

We made it to the forepeak, but the water was already up to our waists. Our only exit was through a small hatch above the forepeak, which could usually be reached by climbing a ladder. Because the ship was on her side, the ladder did not help. The two small hatch doors were jammed tight by the heavy outside water pressure. Bob made it to the hatch first and broke the doors out by sheer strength. The in-rushing water knocked us all away and filled the forepeak in a few seconds.

Bob and Tom managed to work their way back to the hatch and get out; J.C. followed immediately. Tad fought toward the opening; he was not a strong boy. I shoved him from behind, and he made it. The incoming water washed me to one side, and I lost all sense of direction as the water closed over my head. I looked desperately for the hatch but the whole compartment looked the same under water.

I cried out, "Oh God, I'm drowning!"

My words made bubbles as *Albatross* sank, and though I realized I was going to die, I knew there was nothing I could do about it.

Some instinct made me try again to get out. I had a crazy idea about going back the way I had come and trying to escape through a midship skylight. I put out a hand to find the passageway I could not see. The whole ship was full of water now.

You're silly. You can't go back that way. You don't even know where the door is. A ridiculous picture flashed into my mind — the ship was under water and on its side, and I was under water in the ship.

Again I nearly gave up, tasting saltwater in my mouth. This was stupid and unfair. I resented being trapped in a steel hull to die with no chance of escape.

But I wanted a chance, any chance. *Albatross* sank

lower and lower, and as it grew darker, I could no longer think clearly. I was drowning, and I screamed at myself that this is no way to die.

I saw a dim, green light just a few feet away and knew it was a hatch. The ship had changed position and righted herself as she sank. The sails had acted as a rudder, and her ballast-filled steel hull had pulled her upright as she moved slowly beneath the water.

The patch of vague light grew into a milky outline of a hatch. I was too muddled from lack of air to coordinate my movements, but I managed to make feeble sculling motions. Too weak to pull very hard, I exhaled a little to reduce my buoyancy and got one arm through the opening. I was dizzy, verging on unconscious. I did not know which way to move to get to the top. My last clear thought was, "Don't try to swim. Just hold on long enough and you'll rise." I clenched my teeth and hoped I would not open my mouth.

I rose with agonizing slowness through a jungle of lines. The ascent seemed endless, but I was so near to blacking out that I did not even think about getting caught in all those lines.

Something pecked at the back of my head and neck. It was the rain. I lifted my head, gasping at the air, and the gray, squally sky looked terribly bright at that moment. I had the chance I so desperately wanted a minute before. I was back in a world where I could breathe, where I could live.

There was no ship when I looked around at the white-capped seas, no beautiful *Albatross* full of happy boys on their way home from an adventurous cruise. I saw a vegetable crate, some cans and bottles and a lot of floating canvas and pieces of lumber we had been carrying on deck. I could not see the boys who had gone out the hatch ahead of me. Then I realized I had been underwater longer than they, and the wind and waves had pushed them away from the ship.

Albatross' mainmast was over 85 feet high, and though she had righted herself beneath the water, I could see no part it when I reached the surface. Later, some of us estimated I had been carried down over 40 feet inside the doomed ship before I got out. No more than four or five minutes had passed since I'd been reading in a comfortable dry bunk, but in those few minutes our lives had been changed, and some of them had been lost.

I heard a voice shout, "Where's Skipper? Did Alice get out?" Was it possible that anyone was still in the ship? I saw a horrible picture I still can't forget: *Albatross*, undamaged, her white sails set, sinking slowly straight down through hundreds of fathoms of green water, and part of her young crew going all the way down with her.

Downwind, I could see some of the crew hanging to one of the ship's longboats, which was upside down. Chuck's red hair looked orange from the distance, and J.C.'s nearly bald head glistened as he swam toward the capsized boat. I swam toward them, and when I was near enough to be heard I called to J.C. "I didn't think I was going to get out of that."

He shouted back, "You're not out of it yet. Not by a long shot!"

He was right. Until then I had been so busy getting out of the sinking ship that I had not thought about the fact that we were swimming in the open Gulf, a long way from any help. No one on shore even knew what had happened to us.

Was Skipper alive? How many were missing? I made my own count as I swam through the debris. Later I found out that each of us had done the same thing. At first we didn't know who was missing but we all knew quickly that some hadn't made it.

I saw Skipper working at a packaged life raft that had floated up from one of the stern seat lockers. He pulled the lanyard, the CO_2 cartridges were good, and the raft took shape in the water. Skipper ordered a couple of the weaker boys into the raft, and the rest of us got busy on the longboat. I kept thinking of the ship, of what she had meant to all of us, of what she had meant to Skipper and Alice. Then it hit me that Alice was not with us. Skipper had lost his ship, his home and his wife, all within a few minutes. Years of hard work and preparation, years of dreams and anticipation, all were a mile beneath us on the bottom of the sea.

"The sea is one of the great molders of character," wrote Capt. Sheldon in the Ocean Academy brochure. Would eight months of hard work, study and responsibility aboard a sailing vessel really help change a boy into a young man? Chris and Alice thought it would and had tried to prove it. Now we would see the results.

Skipper acted just as a ship captain should; he took command immediately, and we all worked together to empty the longboat. He was calm and sure, and he said nothing about his heavy personal loss.

Suddenly I thought of Spook and shouted his name. One of the boys called to me. "Spook didn't make it, Big Daddy."

It was a hard blow. The sea had claimed him, after all. We would have no more all-night talks on deck. I was close to all who were missing, but I was closest to Spook and knew that it would be a very long time before I should find another friend who could mean as much to me.

The ship's second longboat came to the surface. It had gone far down with *Albatross* but had torn loose from its lashings. Probably we owed that to John, who was mate of the watch when the brigantine sank. He was last seen holding on to the longboat, cutting away at the lines. John was a strong swimmer and could have gotten away, I think, if he had not tried to help the rest of us by freeing the longboat. He must have cut it partially loose, then the boat's natural buoyancy brought it up. No one saw him afterwards.

It was still raining and we were cold, but we had to empty the two longboats somehow. I told Skipper we should try to do it the same way one would right a swamped canoe, in calm water. After righting the first boat we pushed and shoved its bow onto the bottom of the second; that removed about a fourth of the water. Then a couple of the smaller boys slid into the boat over the stern and bailed it out using two plastic buckets that had floated up from the galley. We were lucky to have those buckets; I'm not sure we could have emptied the boats without them. Water kept washing in almost as fast as the boys could bail it out. Finally we got one boat empty enough for half of the boys to get in. They picked up a couple of oars from the water and rowed around through the debris, salvaging anything that might be useful.

The rubber raft helped us empty the second boat. We deflated it partially and shoved it under its bow, which rose and let water run out over the stern. After a few minutes of fast bailing we had the second boat ready for use.

We were colder than we had been in the water. It was still raining, and most of us had no clothing. J.C. and I had underwear and were better off than some. Those who had been on deck watch that morning wore foul-weather gear, so they were able to keep fairly warm. No one wanted to get back into the water to keep warm, though. Sharks appeared, and one glided right by as the last boy climbed over the gunwale.

Skipper had a quick look at the first boat, then moved to the other one. I stayed where I was. We checked our supplies: food was in heavy steel lockers under the seats, and the lockers in my boat had been crushed by the terrific water pressure when the boat was dragged down by *Albatross*. Most of it was all right, though, and the water tank was not damaged. We had enough to last about three weeks if we disciplined ourselves.

No one in my boat was seriously injured. I had hit or somehow twisted my recently broken ankle getting out of the ship, but aside from swelling and throbbing, it did not bother me. I thought of the heavy plaster cast Alice had put on my leg out in the Galapagos Islands and was glad it had been removed two weeks earlier in Panama.

The worst wound was a gash on Bill's head. Our 16-year-old first mate, he had made a harrowing escape by crashing through the galley dumbwaiter that led from the galley down to the main cabin. When *Albatross* capsized, Bill was in the main cabin working out a navigation problem with Chris. Also in the main cabin were Rick, Mike, Tim and Robin. As the water cascaded in through the skylights, the six boys reacted differently. Rick ran for his bunk to try to save the contents. Chris grabbed his camera and started out the aft passageway, which led to the chart house on deck. He wanted pictures of the rough seas, not realizing that *Albatross* would sink in the next minute. Robin scrambled up the steeply angled floor to rescue a pet boa snake he had bought just the week before.

There was no escape for any of the six through the aft passageway.

Even Alice and Spook, who may have been sitting in the chart house when the ship was knocked down, couldn't get out. The steady pressure of tons of sea water against the chart house doors kept them shut despite the attempts of Tod and Chuck to open them from the deck side. The watch did all it could to rescue Alice and Spook, but there just wasn't enough time to do anything except swim.

Those in the main cabin had only one way out: through a narrow passage that led up a ladder from the forward part of the cabin. There was room for only one at a time, and the water was rising rapidly. Mike reached it first, heaving himself up and out after two unsuccessful attempts. Tim followed quickly, but when Bill's turn came, he saw there was so much water pouring down through the passage that it was impossible for anyone else to leave the ship that way. He dove for the 15-inch dumbwaiter shaft. Part-way up, he got stuck and yelled for those behind to push. They did. Rick and Chris were next in line and shoved Bill up through the dumbwaiter. Evidently Chris had re-entered the main cabin when he found the aft exit blocked by water.

Bill broke through the top of the dumbwaiter by using the crown of his head. He came out in the galley after *Albatross* was under water and found the heavy mahogany doors closed. They were jammed, but a blast of air escaping from somewhere inside the ship literally blew him through the doors and into the sea. He floated up through the foreshrouds and reached the surface.

Rick and Chris had no chance to follow him. No one knows what happened to Robin. He was last seen scrambling up the tilted cabin floor to his bunk, crying, "My snake! My snake!"

In the longboats we worked at makeshift sails. Everyone helped, and Mike still had his rigging knife so we could cut lines. With some broken spars and torn canvas and heavy line from the rubber raft we put together a workable sail. The boys in Skipper's boat found one of the regular longboat sails floating in the debris, and they soon had it working. We collapsed the raft and pulled it in to the boat to use for protection from rain and sun; Skipper had a big piece of canvas to serve the same purpose in his boat. I knew that exposure would be our worst problem if we had to stay in open boats very long.

Skipper hailed us and we rowed over to his boat. We had to decide on a heading. He knew our approximate position because he and the boys had been taking regular star sights in the navigation course he had been teaching. We were about 180 miles west of Key West, thus out of the regular shipping lanes.

Skipper thought we could fetch Cuba easily because there was a three-knot current shoving us in that direction, but the chance of being shot on arrival made us decide to head another way. The Bay of Pigs invasion had been over for just a few days when we sank.

We considered trying for the coast of Yucatan, hundreds of miles west, but then Skipper asked me about fishing boats in the Gulf of Mexico. I had lived on the Gulf Coast most of my life and knew that numerous small fleets operated in the area. I suggested we try for the west coast of Florida, thinking we might have a good chance of being picked up by heading north and east.

All of us were reluctant to leave the spot where *Albatross* had sunk; it was hard to accept that the big square-rigger was gone forever and would not rise again. We recognized many of the bits of wreckage floating around us, all objects that we had lived with closely for eight months. I leaned over the gunwale to pick up a few soggy pages of what had been Spook's handwritten recipe book.

Just before we took up our course for Florida, Tim called to Skipper, "Do you think we ought to sail around here a while to see what else we can pick up?" Tim knew we already had whatever we could use; he was actually asking if we should wait to see if anyone else got out. Knowing that Alice was gone, Tim didn't want to ask his question directly.

Skipper understood anyway. He stood up, took a long look all around and said, "No. If anyone else were coming, he'd be here now."

We headed north, setting our course by the cloth charts and an emergency compass in Skipper's boat. Our jury-rigged sail came apart about an hour later. Tim stood on Mike's shoulders to repair it. Despite the cold rain and the pitching boat, they managed to lash it back together, and this time it held. The sharks followed us closely, about six feet astern and keeping pace. We watched their fins glide through the water eight or 10 inches above the surface. One swam over to Skipper's boat, and he hit it on the nose with an oar. All the sharks left soon after that and swam back toward *Albatross*.

The rain stopped early in the afternoon. We ate no lunch, and some of the crew had eaten no breakfast; they slept right through it after coming off watch at 4 a.m. Towards dusk we shared a can of evaporated milk that had been damaged and was leaking. Each took a swallow, and I hammered open a tin of biscuit to eat with the milk. We agreed to drink no water until the next day. The boat pitched around a lot in the rough seas, and it was not safe to stand. I made the boys relieve themselves from a sitting position into a large juice can out of the ship's debris.

I thought we would be picked up in a few days, but in the meantime it was going to be crowded. There were four seats in the 18-foot boats, and with the extra canvas and equipment we had saved, there was not much room. I cautioned the boys to move slowly and carefully one at a time to avoid a fall. A broken bone or bad wound then would have been almost impossible to care for. I tried to work out some duties for the crew to keep their minds occupied. Chuck was made storekeeper and kept track of food and water. Tim and Mike attended to sail and rigging. The other boys were lookouts and were to take turns bailing and steering. Two of us stayed on watch all the time, one to steer and one to handle the sail.

The sail sheet needed constant attention: it had to be let off or drawn in each time a large wave hit us and when the wind changed direction. Steering was difficult because our rudder was broken. We steered with an oar and had to hold it hard over to one side to keep us headed north. We counted on the easterly current to press us toward Florida. The boys took turns steering that first day, and I took over at night.

At dark we tied the boats together to keep from drifting apart, but the long line dragged in the water and slowed our progress, so we untied it. Separated, we made better speed, and when the moon came up, we had clear skies so could see each other all right. We were anxious to stay in sight of Skipper's boat; he had the only compass and charts.

The little clothing we had was wet, but we kept it on for protection from wind and spray. It was impossible to bail the boat entirely dry, and our feet stayed wet. We hoped for sun so we could dry our clothes and get warm. Those on watch wore the few pieces of raingear. The rest huddled together, shivering in the bottom of the boat between the seats under the collapsed rubber raft. It was bulky and heavy, but it kept off much of the cold spray.

About 10 p.m. Chuck thought he saw an airplane, but it turned out to be a satellite. An hour or so later, someone in Skipper's boat saw another light glowing in the distance. It was a big tanker. When he thought she was near enough to see us, Skipper fired a rocket. It had been crushed, though, and went up only 40 or 50 feet. The rocket fell near the boats and we watched it burn on top of the water. The boys' tired, anxious faces shone in the reflected glare. We tried to fire our own rockets but all were water-soaked. Now the tanker was less than a mile away.

Skipper and some of the boys lighted hand flares and waved them back and forth over their heads. The tanker moved gradually away from us.

The boys became very quiet, and no one spoke in either boat. I think they understood for the first time the position we were in, how alone and helpless we were. We heard the lapping of the waves and the creaking of the masts and the rest of the world was silent. Most of us had not expected to be spotted so soon, anyway, but it was depressing to see a ship pass so closely and not see us. Then we heard Skipper say: "Well, that's encouraging. At least we know there are some ships in the area." The boys said nothing. They just watched the fading green light as the ship passed over the horizon.

"Big Daddy! How's this for experience? How about a stroll around the deck and a rum collins at the bar?"

It was J.C. trying to lift the boys' spirits. Some of the crew laughed and we all relaxed again. I had been thinking how alone we were, how insignificant, how remarkable it would be if we were seen. It was appalling to think that our ship was gone, six lives were lost, we were adrift in all that wide sea and no one in the world even knew that any of it had happened.

We talked about the wind that sank us, which Skipper had called a white squall. A hundred years ago, a white squall was a phenomenon known and feared by every seaman, although modern naval authorities say it is probably mythical. Mythical or not, we had been blown down in the water by a force that had given no warning and had not been seen. By the time I reached the surface and looked around for the ship, the violent squall was gone. The sea was choppy and rain was falling, but the tornadic wind had passed. Joseph Conrad writes in *The Mirror of the Sea* about just the kind of sinking we had experienced. He speaks of ships suddenly struck down when least prepared to resist and suggests that instant, violent weather change could be the explanation for the disappearance of many vessels. Had we gone down at night, perhaps none of us would have survived. *Albatross* might have sunk and left no trace, another name on the long list of ships "missing and presumed lost."

Today we know that *Albatross* had probably been the victim of a "micro-burst," or what airplane pilots call wind sheer. Few sailing vessels can survive such a violent burst of wind.

Mike spoke of Coleridge's poem, "The Rime of the Ancient Mariner," which some of the boys had just read in my English class: "The albatross about my neck was hung." The poem will always remind me that an albatross had hung about my neck, too.

I stayed at the steering oar in my boat all night, as did Skipper in his. The boys were not comfortable under the heavy life raft, but at least they were protected a little from the spray and the cold wind that blew constantly. No one complained. They kidded each other, sometimes mentioning things they had lost: clothing, cameras, presents for family and friends. But they could not forget the loss of their shipmates, some of whom had become their strongest, closest friends. No one ever knows how he will react in such circumstances, but I can only praise the way the crew behaved. There was no crying, no whimpering. Each boy willingly did whatever I asked, and I think their morale would have remained high even if we had spent weeks in the longboats. As far as I was concerned, Skipper and Alice had proved the sea is one of the great molders of character.

None of us blamed anyone for the sinking. We all knew that Skipper had done what he could to save the ship and that he was still trying to save us. There was no single careless act that caused *Albatross* to go down. Skipper had tried to shorten sail the instant the blow struck, and as soon as he saw it was too late, he ordered the longboats cut loose. Maybe we were all a little careless or too confident. Each of us had grown to admire the seeming sturdiness of *Albatross*, and she had become our home, a place of safety and security that we never thought might fail us.

Although Skipper was alive, we knew that everything he lived for was dead. Ten years of study, an 18-month voyage around the world on Irving Johnson's *Yankee*, all to prepare himself to bring a dream into reality. On Yankee he met Alice Strahan, who shared the dream and became his wife. Together they sailed the brigantine *Albatross*, the world's only floating high school. The dream was gone.

I marveled at Skipper's composure. He revealed the strain only once when our boats were drifting farther and farther apart. We tried to stay close, but our boat had no rudder, and we simply could not point up into the wind as well as he. We lost sight of the other boat for a minute. Suddenly we heard a shout from Skipper.

"What the hell are you guys doing? Damn it, head her up, Big Daddy!"

"She's up as far as I can get her, and if you think you can do better, I wish to hell you'd try!"

All was quiet for a few seconds. I was sorry I had yelled back and ashamed of having lost my temper. I think the sound of our shouting frightened a few of the boys, but it released frustrations that had been building in both of us. Skipper fell off before the wind and came down nearer to us.

"I'm sorry. I guess you're doing as well as anyone can," he said quietly. His voice seemed small in all that vast space but we were glad to hear it.

Toward dawn I grew very sleepy at the helm. The wind died; we tied up again and drifted together for about an hour. Then the sun rose, the air warmed, and the boys began to stir and stretch. They took off their wet clothes and sat in the sun. We were all very hungry and thirsty, so we decided to eat a few more biscuits and drink a little water. I let one of the boys take the steering oar and moved forward to open the cover on the water tank. My hands were cramped from gripping the oar all night. The cover was jammed, so I banged at it with a hatchet head we found among the boat's tools. As I pounded, I had an odd feeling that I had done the same thing before in the same boat. I had. Eight months earlier in Mystic Seaport, I had helped Alice fill the very water tank I was about to drink from.

Later, as we were hanging up our extra canvas to dry, we heard an excited shout from Skipper's boat. "Ship to starboard!" We looked where he was pointing and saw a big freighter bearing almost straight down on us. We turned the boats quickly and resisted the strong impulse to sail directly toward her. Instead, we sailed at an angle down on her course and crossed her path.

We were very near before anyone on the *MV Gran Rio* saw us. A figure raced along her deck from the stern toward the bridge, waving his arms and looking toward us. We thought she was not going to stop. Finally she slowed, then circled us. My boat was nearest, so we secured our sail and rowed as hard as we could to her side. I saw her captain high above us on the bridge.

"We are from the brigantine *Albatross*," I shouted. "Our ship sank yesterday morning. We have lost six lives."

As I stood in the bow of the longboat trying to explain what had happened, I felt absurd. I was helpless to convey to the captain the dual feeling of grief and hope that had suddenly welled up in me. He asked for our captain and I pointed mutely to the second longboat coming up behind.

"Please repeat what has happened to your ship!"

I was so afraid he would not believe me that I could only point down into the sea and say, "Sank. Sank!"

The captain hesitated and looked from one end of the longboat to the other. Then I heard his order to a deckhand, "Throw them a line." It came flying down from *Gran Rio's* deck, then a rope ladder. I herded the boys up the ladder as fast as I could.

Capt. Frans Vegter and his crew were wonderful. They fed us, let us take hot showers, clothed us, and bandaged our injuries. One of the passengers on *Gran Rio* was Dr. Boyd Arthurs of Ormond Beach, Fla. He dressed the wound on Bill's head and strapped up my ankle. (Dr. Arthurs told me later that Capt. Vegter had intended to radio our position to the U.S. Coast Guard, then go on.)

I watched Skipper as he left us on deck; Captain Vegter had summoned him to the bridge to report the sinking. Skipper's most difficult task was still ahead; he had to explain to the Coast Guard that he had lost his ship and to parents that they had lost their sons.

When we docked at Tampa, Fla., the next day, Skipper was given a batch of telegrams, some from parents of the drowned boys. He handed me one, saying, "I think you'd like to see this one." It was from the father of Chris, who had drowned. I read: "My deepest sympathies are with you now. Thank you for giving our son the happiest year of his life."

White Squall -- Richard Langford

EPILOGUE

Friends and strangers have asked how the experience affected me, about how I feel now after being so near death inside *Albatross*. One thought that comes frequently when I think about the sinking is that pure chance has a tremendous effect on our lives. Where one was standing, how quickly he reacted, determined whether he lived or died.

It was just by chance that we were knocked down in the first place by a freak squall; we might not have been hit had we been 100 feet to one side or the other. The squall hit high in the topsail where, for safety's sake, we flew our oldest, most worn canvas so it would blow out in heavy weather. As chance would have it, *Albatross's* t'gallant sail held and carried her down. Chance saved us from being eaten by sharks after we were in the water. Had they been just a little closer when we sank, we would never have gotten into the longboats. Chance brought *Gran Rio* to our rescue. She had never sailed that route before and did not plan to do so again, but she had a shipment of carnival equipment to unload at Tampa. By chance, Dr. Boyd Arthurs sat down in his cabin after breakfast, looked out a porthole and saw us waving from the longboats.

Chance is not the only controlling factor in one's life, though. One can live by will, also, and can change impending disaster into safety as Bill did by having the courage to enter *Albatross'* dumbwaiter shaft. One can make himself help someone else to escape as Rick and Chris did, even though there was no chance for them. And one can be a ship's captain, lose everything he loves and still find the strength to help the living while grieving silently for the dead.

As I passed *Gran Rio's* galley on my way topside to go ashore, I saw the ship's cook watching me. His round face was serious and did not match the gay mood set by his stiff, clean chef's hat. He beckoned to me with a big wooden spoon he held and spoke softly.

"Do not blame the sea," he said. "The sea will not be the worse for your anger. When you sail the sea, you must take what it gives you. Do not think bad of the sea. I was sunk twice in World War II but I did not get mad at the sea."

I told him I understood and thanked him. I was very tired, my ankle throbbed, I had lost my glasses and was squinting to see. I shook his hand and said good-bye.

On the wharf, speaking to a reporter, Skipper said, "No one can blame the sea; the sea is neutral."

I agree. I feel no bitterness about the sad end to our voyage, just a deep sense of waste and painful loss. Sometimes I dream wishfully of swimming down through fathoms of green water to *Albatross* and finding Spook and Alice and Rick, Robin, Chris and John safe and well. I dream of showing them a way to the surface or a way to bring *Albatross* up with my friends inside. Then I awaken to the real world and understand anew that some of us get through a lifetime and some of us just do not get a chance to try. It is simply the way things are.

A few people such as Spook and Gus are born with an understanding of their own mortality. Most of us don't know we're going to die and do not want to know. I'm one of the lucky few who almost died but got another chance, this time fully believing in and understanding the inevitability of my eventual death.

Why expose yourself to such things? Why go on a voyage in the first place? Why work so hard or be so uncomfortable? Why risk your life daily in such primitive circumstances? The best answer is Thoreau's when he wrote why he went to Walden Pond: "to live deliberately, to front only the essential facts of life, and see if I could not learn what it had to teach, and not, when I came to die, discover that I had not lived."

If one is going to find out who he is, then he must get outside the protective personality of who he thinks he is or who he has been pretending to be.

For a fortunate few, a ship at sea is one of the places where men may front only the essential facts of life as they try to come to terms with the world. On such a voyage as ours, despite its sad ending, if one is very, very lucky, he might find out who he is. And if he does, the world will not be the same again, and life may become the poignant gift that Spook and Gus accepted each day, so happily and gracefully.

Books published by
Bristol Fashion Publications
Free catalog, phone 1-800-478-7147

Boat Repair Made Easy — Haul Out
Written By John P. Kaufman

Boat Repair Made Easy — Finishes
Written By John P. Kaufman

Boat Repair Made Easy — Systems
Written By John P. Kaufman

Boat Repair Made Easy — Engines
Written By John P. Kaufman

Standard Ship's Log
Designed By John P. Kaufman

Large Ship's Log
Designed By John P. Kaufman

Designing Power & Sail
Written By Arthur Edmunds

Building A Fiberglass Boat
Written By Arthur Edmunds

Buying A Great Boat
Written By Arthur Edmunds

Boater's Book of Nautical Terms
Written By David S. Yetman

Practical Seamanship
Written By David S. Yetman

Captain Jack's Basic Navigation
Written By Jack I. Davis

Creating Comfort Afloat
Written By Janet Groene

Living Aboard
Written By Janet Groene

Racing The Ice To Cape Horn
Written By Frank Guernsey & Cy Zoerner

Marine Weather Forecasting
Written By J. Frank Brumbaugh

Complete Guide To Gasoline Marine Engines
Written By John Fleming

Complete Guide To Outboard Engines
Written By John Fleming

Complete Guide To Diesel Marine Engines
Written By John Fleming

Trouble Shooting Gasoline Marine Engines
Written By John Fleming

Trailer Boats
Written By Alex Zidock

Skipper's Handbook
Written By Robert S. Grossman

White Squall - The Last Voyage Of Albatross
Written By Richard E. Langford

Cruising South
What to Expect Along The ICW
Written By Joan Healy

Electronics Aboard
Written By Stephen Fishman

Five Against The Sea
A True Story of Courage & Survival
Written By Ron Arias

Scuttlebutt
Seafaring History & Lore
Written By Captain John Guest USCG Ret.

Catch of The Day
How To Catch, Clean & Cook It
Written By Carla Johnson

Richard E. Landford
Aboard Albatross - 1961

About the Author

Richard E. Langford has lived on and around the sea all his life. Born and raised in Pensacola, Fla., as a teen-ager he served as a volunteer Red Cross water safety instructor and lifeguard. He worked as a professional Safety Services Representative for American National Red Cross, training hundreds of instructors in life saving, swimming, boating, sailing and first aid.

In 1960, he took a leave of absence from Stetson University to serve as English teacher aboard a school ship, the brigantine Albatross. This book is based on its nine-month voyage.

Now retired, Langford writes book reviews and commentary. At age 75, he swims more than half a mile daily in DeLand, Fla.